To Call on His Name

Perspectives on the Jesus Prayer

— JOHN F. GILL —

Sacristy
Press

Sacristy Press
PO Box 612, Durham, DH1 9HT

www.sacristy.co.uk

First published in 2019 by Sacristy Press, Durham

Copyright © John F. Gill 2019
The moral rights of the author have been asserted.

All rights reserved, no part of this publication may be reproduced or transmitted in any form or by any means, electronic, mechanical photocopying, documentary, film or in any other format without prior written permission of the publisher.

Scripture quotations, unless otherwise stated, are from the New Revised Standard Version Bible: Anglicized Edition, copyright © 1989, 1995 National Council of the Churches of Christ in the United States of America. Used by permission. All rights reserved worldwide.

Every reasonable effort has been made to trace the copyright holders of material reproduced in this book, but if any have been inadvertently overlooked the publisher would be glad to hear from them.

Sacristy Limited, registered in England & Wales, number 7565667

British Library Cataloguing-in-Publication Data
A catalogue record for the book is available from the British Library

ISBN 978-1-78959-070-8

*To Clare, Kieran and Gabriel
with love and gratitude*

Foreword

It is one of the great privileges of teaching, and supervising research, that you learn at least as much from your students as you ever teach them. The series of conversations I had with John Gill as he was writing an earlier, more academic iteration of this book was no exception. John Gill has done us all a service by rewriting his research project in a way that makes his thoughts on prayer available and readily accessible to a far wider audience. In doing so, he has refrained from separating scholarship from popular writing, theory from practice, systematic theology from spirituality. He has refused, in other words, to conform to the often constraining disciplinary divisions that have become conventional in Western (but not Eastern) Christian theology.

This book is about a spiritual technique, the Jesus Prayer. It is a model of prayer that has been treasured since the earliest days of the Christian Church and which continues today to be a source of solace and power to those who practise it. In an age increasingly governed by the demands of technology, it is good for us to be reminded of Fr Sophrony Sakharov's warning against reducing the prayer to being *merely* a technical exercise. This book is about a technique, but it never loses sight of the larger purpose, for this is a technique that aims at nothing less than personal encounter, and ultimately mystical union, with God—understood as what John of Damascus called "participation in the divine radiance". "The Jesus Prayer", as our author points out, "is ultimately a means of realizing within ourselves the mystery of *theosis*."

The book considers the theological basis of the Jesus Prayer in the Bible, in patristic anthropology, in hesychast spirituality, and in the Orthodox doctrine of uncreated energies. In discussing the energies the author is careful to correct certain common misunderstandings. The book moves on to consider possible connections with non-Christian traditions of meditation. The distinctively Christian aspect of the Jesus

Prayer lies in its focus on the name of Jesus. The middle part of the book looks more closely at various Western expressions of this focus, with the contemporary movements known as Christian Meditation and Centering Prayer lying at the centre of the discussion. These, and the Jesus Prayer itself, are thus placed in the context of a longer, unbroken tradition in the West as well as the East. The final chapters return to an examination of the Jesus Prayer itself.

To this whole discussion John Gill brings a wealth of understanding, both academic and more personal, and a generosity of perspective that admits of spiritual insights far beyond the boundaries of his own theological background. He has given us a book worthy of careful reading and frequent revisiting.

Duncan Reid
Easter Season, 2019

Preface

The idea of writing this book evolved after I had discovered the Jesus Prayer when reading *The Way of the Pilgrim*, a small book written by an anonymous nineteenth-century Russian author.[1] Despite having read numerous religious and spiritual writings over the years, I had never previously had any knowledge of this prayer practice, which had developed in Eastern Orthodoxy. My reading of this book occurred at a time when I had tried various practices of prayer and Meditation over many years. I had found all of these practices unsatisfactory in various ways, leading to a sense of despondency in regard to spiritual life. Although only a beginner, my hopes were revived when I started practising the Jesus Prayer and learning more about it from the teachings of the spiritual Fathers of the Christian East.

Although raised as a Roman Catholic with an Irish family background, I felt drawn to the Eastern spirituality exemplified by the Jesus Prayer. This led me to the discovery of the Melkite Greek-Catholic Church, which sees itself as a bridge between the Eastern Orthodox Churches and the Latin Church of the West. I discovered that the experience of the Jesus Prayer was expanded and enriched through participation in the liturgical and spiritual practices of the Melkite Church in which I now serve as a deacon.

In my reading, I was surprised to find that there was a dearth of material relating the Jesus Prayer from the East to the prayer traditions of the West. Although vast amounts have been written about each of these prayer traditions, it was difficult to find anything which compared them in depth, exploring their similarities and differences. Furthermore, I was aware that in the latter half of the twentieth century within the Latin Church a widespread dissatisfaction with many of the traditional Catholic prayer practices had developed, leading to experimentation with systems of Meditation, often derived from non-Christian Eastern traditions.

It occurred to me that there was a unique niche for a book which, in addition to providing an overview of the Jesus Prayer in terms of its history, scriptural basis, theology, spirituality, psychology, and practice, also allowed a comparison with the contemplative prayer traditions of the Christian West, including the more recent practices of Meditation. This book is an attempt to contribute to such a perspective in addition to its devotional purpose as an introduction to the Jesus Prayer for readers unfamiliar with it.

This book was written with several groups of readers in mind. Firstly, it is addressed to members of the Eastern Churches, whether Orthodox or Catholic, who may be unfamiliar with this prayer practice which is central to their spiritual heritage. Another important group of readers are people from the Western Churches, whether Roman Catholic or from other denominations, who may also be unfamiliar with this prayer, which can have a universal appeal to all Christians. I hope you will accompany me and find helpful milestones on this journey of discovery.

I also pray that this book will be of interest to readers who are non-Christian or without any religious allegiance. In a world where the reality of God is frequently not recognized, only an experience that touches the heart can effectively indicate his presence. The sincere practice of the Jesus Prayer can give us such an experience, because it is a means of direct encounter with the risen Lord and his divine energies and grace which, with our co-operation, can transform our lives.

This book would not have been possible without the support of my family and friends. In particular, I thank my wife Clare for her support, understanding and forbearance at my many hours diverted from family matters while completing this work.

I thank His Excellency the Most Revd Robert Rabbat, Eparch of the Melkite Catholic Eparchy of Australia and New Zealand for his support of this project. Thank you to my numerous friends in the Melkite community in Melbourne, who have helped in ways they may not be aware of through their friendship and support.

I am very grateful for the generous feedback and advice offered by the Most Revd David Walker, Bishop Emeritus of the Catholic Diocese of

Broken Bay, New South Wales, which has enhanced my understanding of important issues discussed in this book.

I gratefully acknowledge others who have kindly read sections of this text and provided helpful feedback, information, corrections and suggested improvements. In particular, I thank Frs Brendan Byrne SJ, Brian Dunkle SJ, Steve Sinn SJ, Sacha Bermudez-Goldman, Dom David Barry OSB, the Revd Dr Duncan Reid, Tony James and Fouad Ghanem. Any residual errors and defects in this book are entirely my own.

I also offer my sincere thanks to Mr Michael Galovic, the very talented iconographer who has kindly allowed his beautiful icon depicting St Seraphim of Sarov at prayer to grace the cover of this book.

I am very grateful for the kind assistance of librarians associated with the Yarra Theological Union within the University of Divinity in Melbourne, Australia, who have enabled me to find some of the more obscure references quoted in this book. In particular, I thank Ms Miranda Fifield from St Paschal Franciscan Provincial Library at Box Hill, Ms Siobhan Foster from the Patrick Murphy Memorial Library at Box Hill and Mr Philip Harvey from the Carmelite Library at Middle Park.

Contents

Foreword iv
Preface vi
Abbreviations x
Explanatory Notes on Terminology xi

Introduction 1
Chapter 1. What is the Jesus Prayer? 3
Chapter 2. Scriptural Aspects 4
Chapter 3. Patristic Spirituality 20
Chapter 4. Historical Development of the Jesus Prayer 31
Chapter 5. The Indian Connection: Yoga, Mantras and Meditation .. 42
Chapter 6. Monasticism in the West 60
Chapter 7. Christian Meditation 68
Chapter 8. Centering Prayer 77
Chapter 9. The Carmelite Tradition 85
Chapter 10. The Jesuit Tradition 101
Chapter 11. Orthodox Teaching on the Jesus Prayer 109
Chapter 12. Precautions and Controversies 118
Chapter 13. The Jesus Prayer in Context 139

Appendix 149
Suggested Further Reading 152
Bibliography 153
Notes 165

Abbreviations

AC	John of the Cross	*The Ascent of Mount Carmel*
DN	John of the Cross	*The Dark Night*
BL	Teresa of Avila	*The Book of Her Life*
IC	Teresa of Avila	*The Interior Castle*
PG	J.-P. Migne	*Patrologia Graeca*
PL	J.-P. Migne	*Patrologia Latina*
WP	Teresa of Avila	*The Way of Perfection*

Explanatory Notes on Terminology

Throughout this book I have used the term *meditation* with *"m"* in lower-case lettering to refer to the practice of prayerful reflection and discursive thought which is a prelude to prayer and contemplation, particularly in the tradition of *lectio divina*. In contrast, I have used the term *Meditation* with *"M"* in upper-case lettering to refer to various techniques aimed at producing mental states such as heightened awareness, attention, calmness, tranquillity, and wellbeing. *Meditation* in this sense may be used as a spiritual practice associated with prayer, or it may be used for secular purposes such as obtaining psychological or health benefits. I have chosen to arbitrarily differentiate these two meanings in order to avoid what could otherwise be much confusion in referring to the various forms of prayer discussed in this book.

I have used the wording "contemplative prayer" to indicate prayer that leads to inner silence. I have used the word "contemplation" to refer to prayer which is characterized by the experience of mystical gifts conferred as free gifts from God and unachievable by human efforts.

I have made reference to the contrast between *apophatic* and *cataphatic* theology and prayer. Apophatic theology uses negative terminology in reference to God, emphasizing his absolute transcendence, which is beyond anything we can describe or understand. It protects against misrepresentations due to human analogies or anthropomorphisms. Apophatic prayer is directed towards inner silence and receptiveness to God, bypassing our mental faculties of reason, imagination, emotion or memory. Cataphatic theology employs positive statements about God such as his attributes of goodness, love, beauty, omnipotence and omniscience. Correspondingly, cataphatic prayer engages our faculties of reason and thought, memory, will, imagination, feelings and emotions. It comprises verbal or mental prayer, whether personally formulated or standardized, such as the liturgical prayers.

As will be discussed in this book the Jesus Prayer commences as a verbal prayer which may potentially develop into an apophatic cry of the heart under the action of God's grace.

Introduction

This book introducing the Jesus Prayer is written by a beginner for beginners. At the outset, it is important to note that the Jesus Prayer is not simply a technique or something to be practised in isolation. On the contrary, it is a journey into a personal relationship with Jesus, and it becomes an important component of living the Christian life. To produce spiritual growth and transformation the Jesus Prayer needs to bear fruit in Christian living, as well as being integrated into life in the Church community and doing good in the wider world.

I would also like to emphasize that although I am writing to promote the Jesus Prayer and hoping to demonstrate that it encompasses the valuable features of all genuine prayer, I have no intention of disparaging in any way other forms of prayer or suggesting that they cannot be equally beneficial. Nor is there any suggestion that the Jesus Prayer is a magic formula.

In this book, I have drawn upon writings from a variety of sources. As a beginner myself, without any claim to be an expert, I have aimed to present the teachings of various saints and spiritual writers in a way which I hope is convenient and helpful to the reader. In presenting this material, I have tried to let these teachers speak for themselves as much as possible and share with us their wisdom and advice.

I trust that the various references I have listed will guide any interested reader who is seeking more detailed information. I have no wish to "reinvent the wheel", as it were, by replicating the many excellent books written about the Jesus Prayer. Nonetheless, I believe there is a place for a book which attempts to give a multidimensional perspective on the Jesus Prayer and relate it to other forms of Christian prayer. Although the purpose of this book is essentially devotional, an adequate discussion of these multiple dimensions necessarily requires us to take due note of some of the scholarly literature relevant to our theme.

So, Dear Reader, I invite you to join me on this journey of discovery. To start the journey, in chapters 1 and 2 we will examine the wording of the Jesus Prayer and explore its basis in the Scriptures. In chapter 3 we will consider the spirituality of the patristic teachers in the early Christian centuries in the context of the Greco-Roman world following the New Testament period. The era of the Desert Fathers is the background to the historical development of the Jesus Prayer which is discussed in chapter 4.

Our path takes a detour in chapter 5, in which we look at certain Eastern non-Christian traditions of prayer and Meditation in order to better understand them in relation to Christian prayer in general, and the Jesus Prayer in particular. Chapter 6 returns us to the historical road in the West with the rise of Benedictine monasticism and its prayer practice of *lectio divina*. We find that the *lectio divina* pattern becomes an important foundation for much of the subsequent prayer practice in the Western Church, including the Carmelite and Jesuit traditions discussed in chapters 9 and 10 respectively.

Chapter 7 considers Christian Meditation, and chapter 8 looks at Centering Prayer. Both of these modern prayer practices were developed by monks from the Benedictine tradition, who introduced certain innovative changes with apophatic features.

Our path returns to Eastern Orthodox tradition in chapter 11 with important teachings by several eminent Orthodox authorities on the Jesus Prayer and its practice. Words of caution are introduced in chapter 12, because the spiritual path is accompanied by dangers as we approach deeper levels of prayer. This chapter also reviews various controversies relevant to the practice of prayer.

Our journey arrives at its destination in chapter 13, in which the Jesus Prayer is considered in relation to other practices of prayer and Meditation in the West. With its invocation of the Divine Name we learn that it acts like a verbal icon leading us into direct communication with the person of Jesus. I conclude the book with some practical suggestions for any beginner wishing to commence practising the Jesus Prayer. Although in one sense our journey comes to an end at that stage, in a fundamental sense it is also just the beginning, if we commence saying the Jesus Prayer and start to understand the words of the Psalmist who advises us: "O taste and see that the LORD is good" (Psalm 34:8).

CHAPTER 1

What is the Jesus Prayer?

Your name is perfume poured out.
                    Song of Solomon 1:3

The Jesus Prayer developed within Eastern Christianity and is central to the spiritual practices of the Orthodox tradition. It involves repeated invocations to Jesus by name, seeking his mercy. While there is flexibility in the wording of the prayer, the most common formulas in use are:

- "Lord Jesus Christ, Son of God, have mercy on me, a sinner", or
- "Lord Jesus Christ, Son of God, have mercy on me".

The verbal formula can be further shortened to

- "Lord Jesus Christ, have mercy on me/us",
- "Lord Jesus", or
- "Jesus".

The Jesus Prayer can be practised in two ways. A certain amount of time, such as twenty minutes each morning and/or evening, can be set aside on a regular basis, devoted exclusively to repeatedly invoking the Lord Jesus using the words of the prayer. A second, more informal method is to say the prayer silently as often as one wishes at any time when engaged in routine activities, such as when sitting in a bus or going for a walk.

The prayer can be assisted by the use of a rosary-like knotted prayer rope or chaplet (called *komvoschoinion* in Greek and *tchotki* in Russian) as an aid to concentration, with each knot representing one saying of the Jesus Prayer. Holding each knot in turn, between thumb and finger, can help in focusing our attention on directing the prayer to Jesus.

CHAPTER 2

Scriptural Aspects

*The reading of Scripture is manifestly the
fountainhead which gives birth to prayer.*
    Saint Isaac the Syrian[2]

The words of the Jesus Prayer are drawn from the riches of the Scriptures. In this chapter I aim to highlight the biblical basis for the prayer. Let us start our journey by focusing on the scriptural themes which have inspired the historical development and formulation of the Jesus Prayer by spiritual masters of the Eastern Church during the first millennium.

The divine name

The central feature of the invocation of the divine name needs to be viewed against the background of the biblical concept of the power of the name evident in the Old Testament.[3] In the Hebrew tradition personal names were significant and usually expressed a religious belief or prayer of petition. The name of a person was more than a mere identification mark and somehow expressed the personality and nature of the person.[4] In the Hebrew Scriptures "The Name" is frequently used as a substitute for Yhwh himself. He was viewed as being present and active where his name was invoked and to call upon his name was to summon him. The name was therefore to be honoured with great reverence.[5]

The earlier literal understanding of God's presence in the Jerusalem temple in the time of Solomon later became more spiritualized with awareness of the transcendence of God who dwelt in the heavens. The temple was then seen as a house for the *name* of God.[6] In the temple God's presence without containment was expressed as the divine name.[7]

The Hebrew understanding of the name passed into the New Testament, where the name of Jesus is a great power and has a sacramental quality.[8] It has been noted that in the early Christian text *The Shepherd of Hermas* the name of the Son of God was said to be great, boundless and upholding the whole world.[9] In the New Testament the theology of the name is applied to Jesus and testifies to his divinity since "there is salvation in no one else, for there is no other name under heaven given among mortals by which we must be saved" (Acts 4:12).

His name has supernatural power, enabling miracles of healing (Acts 3:6–8) and exorcism of demons (Luke 10:17). Nevertheless, it had to be invoked with faith and any magical power attributed to the name was explicitly rejected, as demonstrated in an episode described in the Acts of the Apostles (19:11–20). The Christological hymn of Philippians 2:6–11 expresses his transcendence over every creature. The preaching of the gospel is described as the preaching of his name.[10] In the Gospel of Luke we are informed that the angel Gabriel declared to Mary that she would bear a son and that "you will name him Jesus" (Luke 1:31). *Jesus* (*Yeshua* in Hebrew or *Iesous* in Greek), a common form of the name Joshua, means "Yahweh saves". Hence the very name of Jesus in itself summarizes the whole of the gospel.

New Testament themes

Let us now consider the New Testament, not from an academic perspective but simply to seek insights about prayer, particularly the Jesus Prayer. From the Gospel accounts of the teachings of Jesus and his day-to-day interactions with people, let us try to ascertain their significance in relation to the Jesus Prayer. As we do this let us keep in mind the wording of the prayer: "Lord Jesus Christ, Son of God, have mercy on me, a sinner." There are some key Gospel themes particularly relevant to the practice of the Jesus Prayer.

Jesus the teacher

Repentance

In Mark's Gospel we read an introductory summary of Jesus' mission, as he proclaims: "The time is fulfilled, and the kingdom of God has come near; repent, and believe in the good news" (Mark 1:15). The central theme of repentance (*metanoia*) is introduced with these words. This Greek word refers to a change of mind and heart. The grammatical wording indicates that Jesus is not referring to a one-off phenomenon but an ongoing process.[11] In other words, as we repeatedly fall away from God we need to just as frequently keep returning to him.

Faith

By introducing the theme of belief in the good news, Jesus also indicates the crucial importance of faith. We notice that repeatedly throughout the Gospels the existence of faith is a crucial factor in the miraculous healings of Jesus. A very notable example is the account of the paralytic man who was lowered through a roof by four men in order to meet Jesus. When Jesus saw the strength of their faith, he pronounced that the sins of the paralytic man were forgiven and subsequently cured him physically as well (Mark 2:1–12; Luke 5:17–26; Matthew 9:1–8). Conversely, we read that when he went to his hometown of Nazareth, he did no mighty works there because of the unbelief of most of the people. On another occasion, when his disciples had been unable to cure an epileptic boy, Jesus stated that it was because of their unbelief and that if one has faith "nothing will be impossible for you" (Matthew 17:20).

Perseverance and patience

Jesus encouraged us to be confident and persevering in prayer when he said: "Ask, and it will be given you; search, and you will find; knock, and the door will be opened for you. For everyone who asks receives, and everyone who searches finds, and for everyone who knocks, the door will be opened" (Matthew 7:7–8). He also said: "So I tell you, whatever you ask for in prayer, believe that you have received it, and it will be yours" (Mark 11:24). Using the example of a man responding to the inconvenient request of a friend in the middle of the night, he emphasized the importance of persistence in prayer (Luke 11:5–8). He went on to teach: "If you then, who are evil, know how to give good gifts to your children, how much more will the heavenly Father give the Holy Spirit to those who ask him!" (Luke 11:13).

In explaining the parable of the sower, Jesus taught that the seed that fell into good soil and produced a rich crop represented "the ones who, when they hear the word, hold it fast in an honest and good heart, and bear fruit with patient endurance" (Luke 8:15).[12] We find that Jesus responds to us by giving us what we need but not necessarily everything that we want. A vivid example is described by Paul in his second letter to the Corinthians. He prayed three times to be delivered from a thorn "given to me in the flesh", but this did not happen. Paul learnt that this affliction was allowed by the Lord "to keep me from being too elated" by the exceptional revelations that he had received (2 Corinthians 12:7–9).

We also note that Jesus did not initially respond to the pleas of the Canaanite woman and acceded to her request only after she exhibited exemplary faith (Matthew 15:28). This lesson is vividly reinforced by the Gospel accounts of Jesus calming a storm on the Lake of Galilee (Matthew 8:23–7; Mark 4:35–41; Luke 8:22–5). Gregory the Theologian referred to this incident when writing about times when God seems to be absent to us: "A voyage at night; no lamp anywhere; Christ is asleep".[13] The terrified disciples, believing they would perish, woke up Jesus, who was asleep in the boat, but as he calmed the storm he chided them for their lack of faith. We can conclude from these examples that Jesus answers our prayers in a manner and at a time that he alone knows is most appropriate for our needs.

Alertness and vigilance

Patient alertness is necessary: "Stay awake and pray that you may not come into the time of trial" (Matthew 26:41). Although Jesus stressed here the importance of vigilance in an eschatological context, his words also remain very applicable to our practice of prayer: "What I say to you I say to all: Keep awake" (Mark 13:37), and "You also must be ready, for the Son of Man is coming at an unexpected hour" (Luke 12:40). The tradition of the Desert Fathers and the later teachers of the Jesus Prayer placed great emphasis on a spiritual aspirant maintaining constant vigilance (*nepsis*) over his or her thoughts so as to maintain the remembrance of God and to instantly repel temptations or hostile distractions.[14]

Prayer and action
Warning against prayer without fruitful action, Jesus stated: "Not everyone who says to me, 'Lord, Lord', will enter the kingdom of heaven, but only one who does the will of my Father in heaven" (Matthew 7:21). On the same theme, in the Gospel of Luke he says, "Why do you call me 'Lord, Lord', and do not do what I tell you?" (Luke 6:46). He then likens the person who listens to his words and acts upon them to one who builds his house on deep, solid foundations that can withstand the force of a flood (Luke 6:47–9).

Prayer in secret
The Gospels speak of Jesus praying alone (Luke 9:18; Matthew 14:23; Mark 6:46). On one occasion "he went out to the mountain to pray; and he spent the night in prayer to God" (Luke 6:12). He taught that prayer should not be performed as a boastful, vainglorious display in front of others, but private prayer should be done in secret: "Whenever you pray, go into your room and shut the door and pray to your Father who is in secret; and your Father who sees in secret will reward you" (Matthew 6:6). He went on to teach that our prayer should not be mere verbiage and meaningless noise: "When you are praying do not heap up empty phrases as the Gentiles do; for they think that they will be heard because of their many words. Do not be like them, for your Father knows what you need before you ask him" (Matthew 6:7–8).

The Lord's Prayer
Jesus taught his disciples what we now call "the Lord's Prayer" (Matthew 6:9–13). It has been described as "the most perfect of prayers".[15] This prayer is deeply embedded in the liturgical prayers of the Church. Although also in general use as a personal prayer, its wording in the first person plural ("Our Father") highlights its prominent function as a communal prayer in contrast to the Jesus Prayer, which is predominantly practised by persons praying individually. In the Lord's Prayer, God is revealed to us by his Son as "Father", and we pray to him in communion

with Jesus Christ his Son in the one Holy Spirit. Referring to the Father as being "in heaven" emphasizes his majesty and glory.

The Lord's Prayer contains seven petitions. The first three represent our movement towards praising and honouring God's glory and will. To pray that his name be honoured as holy is a reminder to us of the biblical significance of the divine name, which in the New Testament is revealed to us as "Jesus". The plea that God's kingdom will come in glory expresses our yearning for the eternal reign of God. Praying that his will be done on earth as it is in heaven expresses our wish for his plan of salvation to prevail for the life of the world.

The last four petitions of the Lord's Prayer focus on our neediness, imperfection and sinfulness. We ask that the Father give us his nourishing daily bread for the needs required in our lives. Our plea for his mercy and forgiveness of our trespasses is linked to our own response to forgive others in turn. We plead that we will not be led into temptation and that we will be strengthened with God's grace to have vigilance and perseverance. And finally, we ask to be delivered from evil, overcoming all that opposes God's goodness.

We might wonder how the Jesus Prayer relates to the Lord's Prayer as taught by Jesus himself. When we consider this question, we soon realize that the Jesus Prayer expresses the same intentions, albeit in a different format. Referring to God as "Our Father" reflects the fact that we have become his adopted sons and daughters through the divine sonship of Jesus. Moreover, Jesus has taught us that "Whoever has seen me has seen the Father" (John 14:9). In the Jesus Prayer we now pray to the Father through the Son. So, in this prayer we venerate the divine name that the Father has revealed.

In the era following the Resurrection and Pentecost we can hallow the Father's name by using the name of Jesus, the significance of which is now apparent. In recognizing Jesus as Lord, Christ and Son of God, we faithfully echo the Lord's Prayer by venerating his name and seeking his kingdom and his will. The petitions in the Lord's Prayer in which we ask for nourishment, healing from sin which is within ourselves, and the overcoming of evil, are all concisely and effectively expressed in the plea of the Jesus Prayer: "Have mercy on me, a sinner."

Forgiveness

In another Gospel passage Jesus emphasized the importance of an attitude of forgiveness when we pray: "Whenever you stand praying, forgive, if you have anything against anyone; so that your Father in heaven may also forgive you your trespasses" (Mark 11:25–6).

Contemplation

In his conversation with the Samaritan woman Jesus tells us more about pure prayer. He speaks of true worshippers who "will worship the Father in spirit and truth, for the Father seeks such as these to worship him. God is spirit, and those who worship him must worship in spirit and truth" (John 4:23–4). This principle of prayer before the face of God that is unobstructed by physical imagery or the limitations of time and place is an important aspect of the Jesus Prayer.

Mystical presence

The incident of the two disciples on the road to Emmaus also introduces the theme of the inward experience of Christ's presence. On the day of the resurrection the two disciples unknowingly converse with Jesus and after he later disappears from their sight they reflect: "Were not our hearts burning within us while he was talking to us on the road, while he was opening the scriptures to us?" (Luke 24:32). The phenomenon of warming of the heart, often mentioned by spiritual writers in relation to the Jesus Prayer, is discussed further in chapter 11.

Mercy

When Jesus reached out to people who were considered disreputable and on the margins of society, he attracted criticism from the Pharisees. In response to the query as to why he ate with tax collectors and sinners, he replied: "Those who are well have no need of a physician, but those who are sick. Go and learn what this means, 'I desire mercy, not sacrifice'" (Matthew 9:12–13).[16] How reassuring this is to us as we approach him for his mercy! Given that the Jesus Prayer is an explicit plea for mercy, there are two Gospel passages which make a special contribution to the biblical foundation of the Jesus Prayer.

The Parable of the Pharisee and the Tax Collector was told as a lesson to those who are proud of their own righteous behaviour, but look down on others. Jesus tells of the two men going to pray in the temple. The Pharisee offered thanks to God that he was morally superior to everyone else, especially the tax collector. In contrast, the tax collector, aware of his unworthiness, stood some distance away. Not daring to raise his eyes to heaven, and beating his breast, he said: "God, be merciful to me, a sinner!" (Luke 18:13). Jesus indicated that the tax collector went home justified with God but the Pharisee did not. "For all who exalt themselves will be humbled, but all who humble themselves will be exalted" (Luke 18:14).

The second passage is the story of the blind beggar Bartimaeus sitting by the roadside, as Jesus and his disciples were leaving Jericho (Mark 10:46–52). Hearing that it was Jesus of Nazareth, Bartimaeus began to shout: "Jesus, Son of David, have mercy on me!" Although many sternly ordered him to be quiet, he cried out even more loudly: "Son of David, have mercy on me!" Jesus called him and after ascertaining that he wanted to regain his sight, he cured him immediately, saying: "Go; your faith has made you well."

God of surprises

The story of Zacchaeus illustrates that God acts in surprising and inscrutable ways. In this incident Zacchaeus, a wealthy and no doubt despised tax collector, had climbed a sycamore tree, possibly out of sheer curiosity, to catch a glimpse of Jesus as he was entering Jericho. Zacchaeus was nonetheless expressing his determination by being prepared to be subject to ridicule due to the indignity of having to climb into a tree. On reaching the spot, Jesus unexpectedly looked up and told Zacchaeus that he would stay at his home that very day. It may be that at that moment Zacchaeus' heart was suddenly touched with repentance, seeing the moral squalor and futility of his way of life up to that point. On the other hand, the use of the present tense in the text suggests that Zacchaeus may have been an honourable person despite his occupation. In any event, he joyfully confirmed that he gave or would give half of his property to the poor and repay fourfold anyone he had cheated (Luke 19:1–10).

This episode highlights the inscrutability of God's merciful actions. It is also noteworthy that this incident expresses both the determined human action of Zacchaeus and the utterly gratuitous and unexpected response of Jesus. This dimension of synergy (*synergia*) between human and divine action is a very important feature in our consideration of prayer and the spiritual life in general.

The compassion of Christ

The miraculous raising to life of the son of the widow of Nain is only recorded in the Gospel of Luke (7:11–16). This miracle is particularly noteworthy in that it did not even occur in answer to a request but out of the spontaneous compassion of Jesus, who was profoundly moved by the terrible plight of the bereaved mother. It was surely the pure expression of his inner nature.

Jesus the Messiah

Jesus is explicitly addressed in the Jesus Prayer as "Christ", that is, "Anointed One" (or "Messiah"). An important moment in the gospel narrative occurs when Peter professes faith in Jesus as the Christ. In Matthew's account he says, "You are the Messiah, the Son of the living God", and Jesus replies that this has not been revealed to him by human agency but by the heavenly Father (Matthew 16:13–17). The incident is also described in the other two synoptic Gospels (Mark 8:27–9; Luke 9:18–21). John's Gospel describes the reply of Simon Peter in response to Jesus asking the Twelve whether they would leave him: "Lord, to whom can we go? You have the words of eternal life. We have come to believe and know that you are the Holy One of God" (John 6:68–9).

Jesus the wonderworker

The Gospel of Mark indicates how even the demons feared and fully recognized the authority and power of Jesus. There are numerous instances of exorcisms by the power of Jesus (Mark 1:23-4; 5:7). All of the Gospels record examples of the saving actions of Jesus with numerous miracles of healing. Going around Galilee, he was "proclaiming the good news of the kingdom and curing every disease and every sickness among the people. So his fame spread throughout all Syria, and they brought to him all the sick, those who were afflicted with various diseases and pains, demoniacs, epileptics, and paralytics, and he cured them" (Matthew 4:23-4). There are also accounts in the Gospels which describe the power of Jesus over the forces of nature (Luke 8:22-5; Matthew 14:22-33).

Jesus as physician of the soul

Of deeper significance than the physical miracles were the cases of spiritual healing and repentance. Chapter 15 of Luke's Gospel relates three parables illustrating God's boundless mercy and joy when we return to him with repentance. In reaction to the criticism from the Pharisees and Scribes about receiving and eating with sinners, Jesus told the parable about the shepherd who leaves ninety-nine of his sheep to seek the one who is lost. Having found it, he rejoices, places it on his shoulders and after arriving home, calls his friends and neighbours to join in the celebrations (Luke 15:4-7). The second parable is of a woman losing one of her ten silver coins. She searches carefully until she finds it and then calls her friends and neighbours to rejoice with her (Luke 15:8-10). The third parable is that of the Prodigal Son who treated his father with contempt, going away and living a dissolute life. Becoming aware of his state of degradation and unworthiness, he repents and returns to his father, who is yearning for his return. He is forgiven and reinstated by his father, who rejoices in his return, much to the resentment of his older brother (Luke 15:11-32).

As well as teaching about forgiveness and mercy, Jesus continually expressed it in his saving actions. Of course, this reached its supreme moment at his crucifixion when he proclaimed: "Father, forgive them; for they do not know what they are doing" (Luke 23:34). A notable illustration of the transformative effects of God's forgiveness occurs in the incident at the home of Simon the Pharisee, where a woman of sinful reputation came in and tearfully kissed the feet of Jesus, wiping them with her hair and anointing them with ointment. Jesus demonstrated to the judgemental Simon that the woman showed such great love because she had experienced forgiveness (Luke 7:36–50).

Jesus, Lord and God

The Jesus Prayer explicitly addresses Jesus as "Lord" and "Son of God". These titles are clearly expressed in the Gospels. The four Gospel accounts all mention the Theophany, which is the revelation of God in the baptism of Christ.

Prior to this event Jesus had lived like an ordinary man but on the banks of the Jordan his divinity was revealed. In Matthew's account, as Jesus came out of the water, he saw the Spirit of God descending like a dove, and there was a voice from heaven proclaiming: "This is my Son, the Beloved, with whom I am well pleased" (Matthew 3:16–17; Mark 1:9–11; Luke 3:21–2). This event is described differently in John's account, where John the Baptist declares that he witnessed the Spirit coming down on Jesus like a dove from heaven, and that it had been revealed to him that the man on whom he saw the Spirit coming down and resting was the one who was to baptize with the Holy Spirit. He added: "I myself have seen and have testified that this is the Son of God" (John 1:34).

Another manifestation of the divinity of Christ is the Transfiguration. In his earthly life this event occurs between his baptism and his passion and death. The Gospel of Mark describes the transfiguration as occurring soon after his first prophecy of the passion (Mark 8:31–3). Taking Peter, James and John up to a high mountain, Jesus is transfigured before them "and his clothes became dazzling white, such as no one on earth could bleach them", and he is seen to be conversing with Moses and Elijah (Mark 9:2–4). From a cloud overshadowing them they hear a voice saying: "This is my Son, the Beloved; listen to him!" (Mark 9:7). In Matthew's account,

Jesus' face "shone like the sun, and his clothes became dazzling white" (Matthew 17:2). Luke's Gospel states that "the appearance of his face changed, and his clothes became dazzling white" (Luke 9:29).

The Johannine perspective

John's Gospel is characterized by a high Christology, emphasizing the divine status and uniqueness of Jesus. It opens with the Prologue stating: "In the beginning was the Word, and the Word was with God, and the Word was God" (John 1:1). It refers to the incarnation of the Word: "The Word became flesh and lived among us, and we have seen his glory, the glory as of a father's only son, full of grace and truth" (John 1:14). It also refers to the unique nature of Jesus: "No one has ever seen God. It is God the only Son, who is close to the Father's heart, who has made him known" (John 1:18). In his conversation with the Samaritan woman, Jesus said: "The water that I will give will become in them a spring of water gushing up to eternal life" (John 4:14). Later, in reply to her mention of the coming Messiah (Christ), he said: "I am he, the one who is speaking to you" (John 4:26). So in the early chapters of John's Gospel we have statements of two titles mentioned in the Jesus Prayer, that Jesus is the *Christ* and the *Son of God*. Jesus makes further claims, including his famous "I am" statements:

> I am the bread of life.
>
> *John 6:35,48*

> I am the light of the world.
>
> *John 8:12; 9:5*

> I am the gate. Whoever enters by me will be saved, and will come in and go out and find pasture.
>
> *John 10:9*

> I am the good shepherd. The good shepherd lays down his life for the sheep.
>
> *John 10:11*

> I am the resurrection and the life.
>
> *John 11:25*

> I am the way, and the truth, and the life. No one comes to the Father except through me.
>
> *John 14:6*

> I am the true vine.
>
> *John 15:1*

In more absolute terms he proclaimed:

> Very truly, I tell you, before Abraham was, I am.
>
> *John 8:58*

In his last meal with his disciples Jesus tells them that it is for their own good that he is going away, and unless he does so the Paraclete ("the Advocate") will not come to them; but if he goes, he will send him to them (John 16:7). In a post-resurrection appearance, he breathes on them and says: "Receive the Holy Spirit..." (John 20:22). The Johannine perspective is encapsulated in the definitive declaration of Thomas to the Risen Jesus: "My Lord and my God!" (John 20:28).

Trinitarian aspects

Both the theophany and the transfiguration are manifestations of the Trinity, featuring the actions of the Father, the Son and Holy Spirit. The transfiguration foreshadows the resurrection of Christ and his victory over death. With his ultimate glorification in the resurrection, Jesus makes appearances to his apostles. At Pentecost his promise to send the Holy Spirit reaches its fulfilment with the birth of the Church. As will be noted in chapter 3, the transfiguration is relevant to the theological debates concerning the nature of grace and the uncreated divine light. The Jesus Prayer is inherently Trinitarian. Although God is transcendent, we can come to know him through his Son, Jesus, the Divine Word of the Father. Jesus had stated: "The Father and I are one" (John 10:30). In the Letter to the Colossians Christ is referred to as "the image of the invisible God" (Colossians 1:15). Jesus himself stated: "Whoever has seen me has seen the Father" (John 14:9).

While Jesus is addressed by name in the Jesus Prayer and the reality of God the Father is indicated through Jesus being invoked as "Son of God", there is no explicit mention of the Holy Spirit. Nevertheless, the Spirit is necessarily present. "No one can say 'Jesus is Lord' except by the Holy Spirit" (1 Corinthians 12:3).

While Jesus leads us to the Father, the Holy Spirit proceeds from the Father, sent by Jesus and leading us to Jesus. Preparing the way, the Spirit precedes him.[17] In the biblical account of the creation, the Spirit is described as sweeping over the face of the waters before God announces: "Let there be light" (Genesis 1:3). In like manner, he was present to the Virgin Mary with the announcement by the angel Gabriel: "The Holy Spirit will come upon you, and the power of the Most High will overshadow you" (Luke 1:35).

Pauline teachings

In addition to assuring us that we confess Jesus as Lord only through the Holy Spirit (1 Corinthians 12:3), Paul also told us that: "The Spirit helps us in our weakness; for we do not know how to pray as we ought, but that very Spirit intercedes with sighs too deep for words. And God, who searches the heart, knows what is the mind of the Spirit, because the Spirit intercedes for the saints according to the will of God" (Romans 8:26-7). He urged us to: "Pray in the Spirit at all times in every prayer and supplication" (Ephesians 6:18). He also wrote: "Persevere in prayer" (Romans 12:12) and "Devote yourselves to prayer, keeping alert in it with thanksgiving" (Colossians 4:2). A very important Pauline statement relevant to the Jesus Prayer is: "Pray without ceasing" (1 Thessalonians

5:17). As will be discussed in describing the history of the Jesus Prayer, this instruction came to be understood by many in quite a literal manner in the practice of this prayer.

Conclusions

This brief overview of themes from the New Testament has revealed the deep scriptural significance of the words of the Jesus Prayer. The invocation of the *Name of Jesus*, addressing him by his titles of *Lord*, *Christ*, and *Son of God*, expresses faith in him and acknowledges his exalted divine status. It is also apparent that the prayer is inherently Trinitarian, being directed through Jesus to God the Father by the action of the Holy Spirit.

The *plea for mercy* closely mirrors the Gospel accounts of the Parable of the Pharisee and Tax Collector and the cry for mercy of the blind beggar Bartimaeus. In this way the prayer illustrates the crucial importance of humility, profound repentance, faith and perseverance in our quest for God's saving grace. The words of the tax collector are penitential, asking for God's mercy and forgiveness, while the words of Bartimaeus are a plea for light and illumination.

The Gospel descriptions of the teachings of Jesus also give us many lessons to guide both our practice of prayer and the Christian life in general. The teachings about praying in secret emphasize the importance of contemplative prayer. In this prayer we withdraw from outward concerns and move towards inner stillness, in which we remain vigilant and receptive to God's presence enveloping us in the silence. Jesus also taught us the necessity of being in a state of peace with a forgiving heart towards others when we pray, in order to receive God's grace and mercy despite our own failings. He taught us the need for fruitful action, so that prayer is not limited to mere words. The Gospels illustrate his great emphasis on the crucial need for faith, humility, repentance and patient perseverance.

The Gospel accounts of the actions of Jesus convey powerful messages relevant to the Jesus Prayer. The many instances in which Jesus worked both physical and spiritual miracles and wondrous healings give witness to his glory and divine power. These aspects are acknowledged in the titles of *Christ, Lord* and *Son of God* used in the Jesus Prayer.

The case of the woman with a haemorrhage who was cured instantly after simply touching the hem of his garment is especially noteworthy. It is significant in this incident that Jesus referred to the fact that he could feel power going out from him (Mark 5:30). This foreshadows later theological understandings of the divine, uncreated energies. This account of the dramatic cure of a desperate but faith-filled woman reminds us of the need for energy to acquire healing and transformation. It suggests that reaching out to Jesus in faith and prayer will invite his response, conveying the grace and energies that we require.

That the miracles of Jesus were typically in response to the faith of the recipients illustrates the significance of synergy in which human effort combines with God's grace to work wonders. The Gospels are replete with instances of people finding transformation through their encounters with Jesus. In the Jesus Prayer we seek such a direct meeting with the Lord. Can we doubt that if we encounter the presence of Jesus in our hearts in prayer, he is any less accessible to us or willing to visit us with his grace than he was with the people we read about in the Gospels whom he healed and transformed? These reflections give us hope that if we practise prayer in the same spirit as that described in the Gospel examples, it will nurture within us a relationship with Jesus, who through the Holy Spirit leads us to his Father. Living in our hearts, he will guide us in his way and share with us his cross, resurrection, and ultimately, the joy of his kingdom.

The Pauline teachings speak to us about the Holy Spirit praying within us. Paul's instruction to "pray without ceasing" (1 Thessalonians 5:17) has inspired the tradition of seeking constant union with God in the prayer of the heart, which has been central to the historical development of the Jesus Prayer. The Jesus Prayer can in no way be seen as manipulating or demanding God's grace or his presence. Nonetheless if practised sincerely with faith, sincerity, humility and a spirit of repentance it can prepare us by making us open and receptive to God's grace and action within us. We can thus be reassured by the words of the Son of Man: "Listen! I am standing at the door, knocking; if you hear my voice and open the door, I will come in to you and eat with you, and you with me" (Revelation 3:20).

CHAPTER 3

Patristic Spirituality

The kingdom of heaven is like treasure hidden in a field.
Matthew 13:44

We now proceed to a brief review of some of the key spiritual teachings of the Eastern Church Fathers. This helps us to understand some of the philosophical, psychological and theological dimensions to the practice of the Jesus Prayer. Their insights into human nature and the spiritual path are also important in understanding the tradition of hesychasm in which the Jesus Prayer is practised by the monks of Mount Athos and other monastic centres. Knowledge of these themes is relevant to the discussions in later chapters in this book concerning the processes involved in spiritual life and prayer. Familiarity with the terminology used by the patristic and early Christian writers is also important to understanding Eastern spiritual literature such as *The Philokalia*.[18]

Body and soul

The Fathers teach that the human being is neither a body nor a soul in isolation but a union of both together. On the one hand, they rejected the spiritualist approach of Gnosticism and Platonism, which view the body as being a prison or tomb for the soul. On the other hand, they also rejected a materialism which reduces the soul to a mere epiphenomenon of the body.[19] Irenaeus wrote that human beings are "compound by nature, and made up of body and a soul".[20]

Symeon the New Theologian taught that the soul is united to the body "in an inexpressible and indetectable way, and blended without mixture or confusion".[21] Evagrius of Pontus recognized that changes in the body produce thoughts and ideas in the soul.[22] On the other hand, Maximus the Confessor taught that

> the body is an instrument of the intellectual soul of a man, and the whole soul permeates the whole body and gives it life and motion. At the same time, the soul is not divided or enclosed within it, since the soul is simple and incorporeal by nature. It is wholly present to the entire body and to each of its members. The body is of such a nature that it can make place for the soul by an inherent power that is receptive to the soul's activity.[23]

The body needs the soul to live and move; the soul needs the body to manifest, express itself and act on the external world.[24] Using the conceptual framework of Greek philosophy, some of the Fathers referred to *powers of the soul* expressed at three levels.[25] The most elementary, vegetative level is possessed by all living beings. This power reflects the basic life principle allowing nutrition, growth and generation. The second level, common to both humans and animals, reflects non-rational elements, particularly the features of appetite/desire (*to epithymitikon*) and the incensive power/irascibility (*to thymikon*) from which arises spirited and vehement feelings. The third level is the power of reason that is characteristic of human nature. The principal faculties at this level are: discursive thinking and logic (*dianoia*) and the highest faculty, the contemplative/intuitive (*nous*) or spirit (*pneuma*). All the intellectual functions, including will and self-determination, occur at the third level. The modern concept of *the mind* includes features at both the second and third levels.

Gregory of Nyssa taught that the soul "is stationed like a guard" over each element of the body.[26] The rational soul is capable of ruling the irrational elements of irascibility, desire and everything connected with affections and imagination.[27] The soul is essentially independent, even though it uses the body as an instrument and depends upon it to manifest its activities in the exterior world. It can transcend the limits of the body and continues to live even after death.[28]

Body—soul—spirit

Jean-Claude Larchet claimed that the Fathers frequently used the dichotomous body–soul model, but on occasion a tripartite spirit/intellect–soul–body model was used.[29] Both of these schemes, which have precedents in classical thought, are also found in Paul. Archbishop Chrysostomos has argued that notwithstanding certain scriptural and patristic passages which seem to support a tripartite understanding of the human composite, the Greek Fathers saw the things of the mind or intellect as higher faculties of the soul and not a separate third element. Thus, when Eastern Orthodox theologians speak of body, soul and spirit (or mind), they nonetheless accept the dichotomous nature of the human being.[30] There is a hierarchy of interaction whereby the soul, because it is immortal and immaterial, is superior to the body, which in man's fallen state is material and mortal.

Larchet has noted a further source of possible confusion in the terminology. For authors in the first centuries the word *pneuma* was used in the sense indicated by Paul (1 Thessalonians 5:23), but the Fathers of the fourth century and the Byzantine Fathers of later centuries used the word *nous* with the same meaning.[31] This latter word is frequently used in relation to hesychasm and the Jesus Prayer. It is seen as the highest human faculty, expressing the capacity for self-determination and relating to God. It is often seen as the image of God in human beings.

Psyche

The word *psyche* used in the Scriptures is usually translated as "life" or "soul", but, while generally suggesting dematerialized existence, it has various shades of meaning.[32] It refers to the animating life-principle. It can also have the sense of "person" or "individual". It can approximate the concept of "self". In the Pauline texts the meaning of the words *psyche* and *pneuma* can be hard to differentiate.[33]

Pneuma

The earliest meanings of *pneuma* were "breath" and "wind". As "breath" it indicates the life principle. In the New Testament *pneuma* nearly always refers to supernatural influences.[34] It can refer to the spirit or higher nature in man. It can refer to non-corporeal beings, or the Spirit of God, or God's being as a controlling influence.[35]

The *nous*

Although the earlier meaning of the word *nous* as used in the New Testament refers to the intellectual faculty, the mind, thinking or reason, it later changed to indicate a higher spiritual faculty.[36] John of Damascus taught that the *nous* is the purest part of the soul (*psyche*): "As the eye is to the body, so is the *nous* to the soul."[37] Although it can be distorted by sin, it cannot be destroyed. Through grace it is created immortal, and through grace it has the possibility, along with the whole human composite, of becoming transformed in deification. According to Lossky, the *nous* is "that contemplative faculty by which man is able to seek God . . . ", and "it might be said that it is the seat of the person".[38] The *nous* is not external to the body. On the contrary, the entire soul, including the *nous*, is blended with the body and totally penetrates it. In the words of Larchet:

> By this total union of the *nous* to the totality of soul and body, the entire man is made in the image of God and as a result is a hypostasis. By this union, the body and soul receive the possibility of complete participation in the spiritual life. The *nous* has the power to bring all the other elements of the human composite under its control and of inducing them to conform to itself, to spiritualize them and communicate to them in their inmost being the divine energies which they, by their nature, are capable (*dektikos*) of receiving. It is through the medium of the *nous* that the totality of man is capable of being one with God and being deified.[39]

The heart

The Eastern Fathers followed the traditional biblical understanding of the heart (*kardia*) as our principal organ, physical and spiritual. The prophets had urged a return to the heart, to change it from a heart of stone into a heart of flesh. The word "heart" should not be understood only in its ordinary sense but in the sense of "the inner person".[40] The heart is the deepest centre of the person. It is:

> the spiritual center of a man's being, man as made in the image of God, his deepest and truest self, or the inner shrine, to be entered only through sacrifice and death, in which the mystery of the union between the divine and the human is consummated ... 'heart' has thus an all embracing significance: 'prayer of the heart' means prayer not just of the emotions and affections, but of the whole person, including the body.[41]

The fall and restoration

The Fathers considered that the present state of humanity reflects fallen human nature, explicable in terms of the ancestral sin. Gregory Palamas spoke of the consequence of this sin as spiritual death of the soul in separation from God. Following on from this estrangement from God, illness and physical death followed.[42] Nevertheless, although the image of God was tarnished, humans were not wholly deprived of the potential for restoration. The Greek Fathers saw the path of salvation as a process of healing which leads to deification (*theosis*).[43] John of Damascus saw the state of *theosis* as "participation in the divine radiance" (*metoche tes theias ellampseos*) but not "the divine essence" (*ten theian ousian*).[44]

Humanity becomes restored through the grace of Christ who, in the famous words of Athanasius "was made man so that we might be made God".[45] The incarnation and the resurrection herald this restoration of human nature. The Orthodox tradition also emphasizes that the whole person, including the body, shares in the process of deification. A process of cleansing of the mind and body involves three steps: purification, illumination and, ultimately, deification (or glorification). Even in this present life we can gain a foretaste of the future glory of God's kingdom.

The apophatic Christian tradition recognizes that God in his transcendence is completely Other, beyond our understanding and beyond Being itself.[46] Therefore the Eastern Fathers were wary of using merely human concepts in discussing spiritual realities. Scripture states: "No one has ever seen God" (John 1:18) and God dwells in "unapproachable light" (1 Timothy 6:16). Nonetheless, while his essence is unknowable to us, he is considered to be accessible to us in his energies. Accordingly, Athanasius wrote: " . . . as being in all creation, he is in essence outside everything but inside everything by his own power".[47]

Hesychasm

Practised most famously by the monks of Mount Athos, hesychasm takes its name from the Greek word *hesychia*, which means "silence" or "stillness". The silence which is sought is not merely the absence of noise, but silence filled with the divine presence. It is a mystical tradition based on focusing attention within the depths of one's being while repeating the Jesus Prayer.[48] It has been called "a system of Christocentric mysticism and of a spiritual lifestyle, and psychosomatic prayerful practices", seeking inner silence and communion with God.[49]

In quoting another unnamed spiritual master, Isaac the Syrian referred to the transformational capacity of *hesychia*: "Stillness cuts off the occasions and causes that renew thoughts, while within its walls it makes the memories of predispositions grow old and wither. And when this old material wastes away in the mind, the understanding returns to its own nature and directs it".[50]

The theology of hesychasm

Gregory Palamas in the fourteenth century defended hesychasm, seeing it as an expression of the patristic tradition. In the words of George Habra, a Melkite Catholic writer:

the doctrine of Palamas is but the 'organic' development of earlier doctrines, differing from them only in that, while these are very rich intuitions, Gregory has given us a more philosophical and dialectical elucidation of the content.[51]

The controversy regarding hesychasm was instigated by a Calabrian monk named Barlaam and represented a confrontation between the traditions of the Christian East and the rising influence of Scholasticism in the Christian West. Barlaam was scandalized by the hesychastic practices on Mount Athos which he witnessed, and he criticized the physical exercises associated with them. He alleged that it was believed that these practices would allow one to see the essence of God, thereby constituting the heresy of Messalianism, which taught that the persons of the Trinity could be visible to the human eye.

Gregory Palamas wrote treatises in defence of the hesychasts, known as his *Triads*. He argued that both in this world and in the next, humankind can share in the divinity through God's uncreated energies. He considered that spiritual knowledge does not come through worldly education but through the radiance resulting from cleansing of the mind and heart and the attainment of holiness and virtue. He asserted that in arguing that the mind should be free from the body in prayer, Barlaam had contradicted the Pauline doctrine that the body is the temple of the Holy Spirit (1 Corinthians 6:19). When cleansed from sin and purified from passions, the mind functions in harmony with the body.[52]

Archbishop Chrysostomos has outlined some of the main themes of the Palamite teachings: when the *nous* returns the mind to the heart, the heart exerts control over thoughts and the mind becomes "watchful". Certain physical exercises such as coordination of breathing with the rhythmic saying of the Jesus Prayer can aid this process. Gregory argued that the body must participate actively in prayer and he suggested concentration of the mind on the centre of the body or on a candle in stillness to remove distractions during the Jesus Prayer. The attainment of pure prayer involves an encounter with God in the heart. Pure prayer ultimately leads to the vision of God manifesting as uncreated light (*aktiston phos*) or the divine radiance (*theia ellampsis*). Gregory maintained that this is the same light which Christ manifested at the

Transfiguration on Mount Tabor and which Paul experienced on the road to Damascus. Uncreated light floods the mind with grace so that the *nous* is totally cleansed.[53]

In response to the allegations of Messalian heresy, Gregory drew a distinction between the *essence* and the *energies* of God. He emphasized that the hesychasts do not seek a physical vision of the transcendent and unknowable essence of God and nor do they claim that the uncreated light is his unknowable essence. On the contrary, the uncreated light is a manifestation of the energies of God perceived by the *nous* and also, potentially, by the senses when they are purified, transformed and illuminated. This reconciles God's transcendence, which is beyond our knowledge, and his immanence, whereby he reveals himself to us through his energies.

Gregory also answered the further objection that the uncreated energy introduced a second or lower God beside the unique Godhead. He taught that no multiplicity of divine manifestations could affect the unity of God, who is without any division into parts, or prevent him from revealing himself wholly in each of these energies. The divine energies are not created things but a manifestation of the existence of the living God.[54]

Melkite Catholic Archbishop Joseph Raya (1916–2005) has described the Palamite doctrine of the divine energies as follows:

> It is not God's action but God himself in his action who makes himself known to man and gives him the ability to "see" him. God enters into man's love, remaining there in his intimate reality. This presence is real, indeed most real. This communication of God himself is called "Uncreated Energy". The uncreated energies of God are not "things" which exist outside of God, not "gifts" of God; they are God himself in his action. They are the very God who is himself Uncreated. They are therefore called "uncreated" because their cause and origin is the Essence of God. In them God, as it were, goes beyond himself and becomes "transradiant" in order to really communicate himself.[55]

Archbishop Chrysostomos considers that Barlaam could not understand the hesychasts, because their spiritual lives and practices were not a matter of speculative theology but of spiritual experience. The hesychasts in turn viewed some Western ideas as deviating from the empirical experience of the Greek Fathers and not aimed at the restoration of man to the image of God. The difference between Barlaam and the Palamites was therefore the difference between intellectual knowledge of God and religion as a "therapeutic way of life".[56]

The hesychasts engaged in ascetic observances to separate themselves from the passions and mental distractions which clouded the mind. Their practices included fasting, vigils, prayer, good works, observing the commandments, and life centred on the mysteries of the Church, particularly the Eucharist.[57]

In discussing the theology of hesychasm, John Meyendorff (1926-92) noted that Barlaam based his position on two postulates derived from Greek philosophy. Firstly, there was the Aristotelian teaching that all knowledge was derived from sense perception. Secondly, there was the Neoplatonic principle that since God is beyond sense experience and therefore unknowable, all knowledge of him must be indirect and always passing through sense perception. Palamas could not accept Barlaam's naturalistic thought, which denied the possibility of direct intervention of the spirit in man's knowledge of God.[58] In contrast, he taught a doctrine of supernatural knowledge which is independent of sense experience but granted in Jesus Christ to the whole person, body and soul, admitting him even while on earth to the first fruits of final deification and the vision of God, not through his own power but by the grace of God.

Meyendorff argued that Gregory Palamas, in defence of the psychophysical methods of hesychasm, held to a biblical view of the human being in which the body, far from being a prison for the soul, itself receives the grace of the sacraments and the inheritance of a final resurrection.[59] Since the incarnation of the Word, our bodies have become temples of the Holy Spirit who dwells in us (1 Corinthians 6:19). We must seek the spirit in our own bodies, sanctified by the sacraments and engrafted by the Eucharist into the body of Christ. Christ is no longer exterior to us but now found within us as living members of his body, the Church.[60] Gregory argued that

> the spiritual joy which comes from the mind into the body is in no way corrupted by the communion with the body but transforms the body and makes it spiritual, because it then rejects all the evil appetites of the body; it no longer drags the soul downwards but is elevated together with it.[61]

Thus, in contrast to Hellenistic philosophy, he reaffirmed the dignity of matter rather than seeing matter and spirit in opposition to each other. The grace of baptism and the Eucharist has already given the Christian new life contained within his or her own being. Hesychasm is reliant on the historical facts of the incarnation of the Word and the resurrection. The second coming of Christ is already a reality in sacramental life and spiritual experience but awaits its full manifestation in the future glory of the heavenly kingdom.[62]

The patristic and hesychastic traditions have been briefly discussed in this chapter not merely out of historical interest, but because they bring to light important issues relevant to practising the Jesus Prayer. An anonymous author has written that the spiritual tradition of the Christian East has become focused almost exclusively on a specific method and tradition of prayer: viz. "The Prayer of the Heart"; "The Jesus Prayer"; or Hesychasm.[63] He has pointed out that these three terms refer to the same thing but highlight different aspects of it: "The Prayer of the Heart" emphasizes *the method*; "The Jesus Prayer" stresses *the words* of the prayer; and "hesychasm" is a convenient description of *the school of spirituality* which has arisen from the prayer. The Jesus Prayer is not merely a practice but rather a complete approach to the whole of Christian life.[64]

John Romanides (1927–2001) has suggested that Orthodoxy is not simply a religion like all other religions, and it is not merely concerned about lower-level doctrinal matters. It is a therapeutic science. In his words: "Doctrine is not what saves people. It simply opens the pathway for man to reach purification and illumination".[65] He considered that the core concern of the Church is to provide healing through "the three stages of spiritual ascent: *purification* from passions, *illumination* by the grace of the Holy Spirit, and *theosis*, again by the grace of the Holy Spirit".[66]

He taught that thoughts belong to our reasoning faculty (*dianoia*) and should not be present in the *nous*. He maintained that spiritual healing requires the *nous* to be emptied of all thoughts whether they be good or bad. In this way it remains pure and thus receptive to the indwelling of the Holy Spirit. The Holy Spirit can then pray ceaselessly within the heart. In noetic prayer a person feels someone else, the Holy Spirit, praying within his heart with "sighs too deep for words" (Romans 8:26). The body is thus a temple of God because the Holy Spirit has come and taken up his abode in the heart. Paul wrote of the Spirit of God crying within our hearts: "Abba! Father!" (Galatians 4:6). A state of illumination occurs when unceasing noetic prayer becomes active within the human heart.[67] Romanides has stated: "The mind (*dianoia*) keeps an eye on the prayer of the heart but it does not participate in it using the forms of rational thought. It simply eavesdrops on the Holy Spirit's prayer in the heart. This is what is meant by the Holy Spirit praying in the heart."[68] In the ultimate state of *theosis* the *nous* becomes fully healed and purified.

CHAPTER 4

Historical Development of the Jesus Prayer

Remember the days of old, consider the years long past; ask your father, and he will inform you; your elders, and they will tell you.
Deuteronomy 32:7

The early Church Fathers made a variety of interpretations of Paul's instruction to "pray without ceasing" (1 Thessalonians 5:17).[69] One approach was to observe set times for prayer during the course of the twenty-four hours of the day and night. In this way the whole day was seen as sanctified. A second approach was to include good actions within the category of prayer. A third approach was advocated by Augustine, who recommended an unceasing prayer of desire. In a homily commenting on Psalm 38:9 (37:9 LXX) he taught:

> This very desire of yours is your prayer; and if your desire is continual, your prayer is continual too. It is not for nothing that the Apostle said: *Pray without ceasing.* Can we unceasingly bend our knees, bow down our bodies or uplift our hands, that he should tell us: *Pray without ceasing?* No; if it is thus he bids us pray, I do not think we can do so without ceasing. There is another way of praying, interior and unbroken, and that is the way of desire. Whatever else you are doing, if you long for that sabbath, you are not ceasing to pray. If you do not want to cease praying, do not cease longing. Your unceasing desire is your unceasing prayer.[70]

Notwithstanding this teaching, Augustine also advocated the practice of set prayers at times throughout the day as a means of stirring up the unceasing desire for God.[71]

The fourth approach was that adopted by the Desert Fathers, who held to the ideal of constant prayer in a more literal sense. In the Christian East this approach ultimately led to the development of the Jesus Prayer. Our next task is to follow the story of how this tradition led to the Jesus Prayer in its present form. The Jesus Prayer was developed in a lengthy process extending from the time of Antony in the third century. The Old Testament tradition of reverence for the Divine Name was expressed in the New Testament by veneration of the Name of Jesus. Notwithstanding its power, to be efficacious the invocation of the Name of Jesus required genuine faith.[72]

The early centuries

In general, the early Christian believers did not use the name "Jesus" by itself without adding titles such as *Kyrios* (Lord) or the messianic name *Christos* (Messiah), expressing their faith, respect and love.[73] In both the New Testament and in the writings of the Apostolic Fathers the most common invocations to Jesus included the title *Kyrios*.[74]

Although the words of the Jesus Prayer are present within the four Gospels in fragmentary form, there is no documentary evidence from the first century to show that they were synthesized into the final formula at that stage.[75] The liturgical formulas most frequently used were acclamations of praise to the Lord.[76] Prayers for help and protection were initially more common than pleas for mercy.[77] The titles used by the early Christians had doctrinal significance in dealing with heresies. Reference to the "Lord", "Jesus Christ", "Son of God" or "Saviour" had doctrinal significance as professions of faith in Christ as God. According to Hausherr, Syriac-speaking Christians, in comparison to the Greeks, always used the Name of Jesus with greater familiarity.[78] To "call on the Name of the Lord" did not simply mean pronouncing the name "Jesus", but rather expressing adoration of Christ as God.[79]

Evagrius of Pontus

Macarius of Egypt (c.300–c.390), few of whose works have survived, appears to have been one of the first teachers of the use of short prayers invoking the Lord by Name. He was a teacher of Evagrius of Pontus (346–99), a monk who, influenced by Neoplatonism, advocated apophatic, non-discursive, imageless prayer. Evagrius emphasized prayer consisting of immaterial contact of the intellect with God.[80] For him, pure prayer meant "a laying aside of thoughts" (*apothesis noematon*).[81] Pure prayer in the Evagrian sense could not be practised as an habitual or constant state.[82] Evagrius did not record a practical method to achieve such prayer.

The early monks of the desert in following the advice of Paul (1 Thessalonians 5:17) sought to engage in continual prayer through remembrance of God by using a variety of very short "arrow" prayers, usually comprising either one word or a brief phrase from a psalm repeated frequently. Initially there was much flexibility in the actual words used in their prayers.[83] It was recognized that what counted was the interior disposition rather than the formula of words. Asceticism and spiritual combat were needed to overcome the forces seeking to divert their attention from God.[84]

An unknown author in the fifth century, called Pseudo-Macarius, represented a more biblical perspective of the total person than that of Evagrius. He emphasized the union of body, mind, and soul centred in the heart.[85] He taught that: "In the heart, the mind abides as well as all the thoughts of the soul and all its hopes. This is how grace penetrates throughout all parts of the body."[86] In the development of the Jesus Prayer can be seen a synthesis of the approaches of Pseudo-Macarius and Evagrius in the phenomenon of "Mind in the Heart".

There are Egyptian texts preserved in Coptic which explicitly refer to the practice of the Jesus Prayer. They purport to contain sayings of Macarius which, if correct, would establish that the Jesus Prayer was familiar to monks in fourth-century Egypt. There is, however, good evidence that they date from around the beginning of the period of the Arab domination (second half of the seventh century or first half of the eighth century).[87] It may be that they used the name of Macarius because of his prestige and authority. These texts clearly indicate an advanced stage in the development of the Jesus Prayer. They contain mention of the invocation of the saving name of Jesus said with compunction and with an appeal for help and mercy, the invocation being continuous and made with every breath.

Stress is laid on the "sweetness" experienced with the invocation. The name of Jesus is described as a nourishment and very sweet food.[88] There is mention of praying with the use of no representation or form, the whole activity focused on simple attention.[89] The texts contain elements of varied origin. Some of the material is likely to derive from the words of Macarius himself but other material describing the Jesus Prayer probably belongs to a later period.[90] Compunction, mourning and sorrow for sin also became an important element in the development of the Jesus Prayer. In this way, the whole monastic spirituality of compunction was condensed into one short formula as a means of attaining continual prayer.[91]

Saint John Cassian

John Cassian (c.365–c.435) was a very important figure linking the Eastern and Western churches. He appears to have been born in the Latin-speaking area of what is now Romania. He later lived as a monk in Bethlehem, subsequently meeting and learning from Spiritual Fathers in Egypt before finally setting up monastic foundations in what is now France. He wrote about what he had learnt from the Desert Fathers, and in his work *Conferences* he elaborated important teachings on prayer.[92] His work was acknowledged by Benedict of Nursia, and he was a significant influence on the later Benedictine monastic tradition.

He pointed out the necessity of virtue, humility, simplicity and the overcoming of vices and passions as prerequisites for a monk acquiring progress in prayer.

In *Conference 9*, Cassian recounted the words of Abba Isaac that after prayer with supplication, pleas, and thanksgiving, "a state of soul more exalted and more elevated will follow upon these types of prayer. It will be shaped by the contemplation of God alone and by the fire of love and the mind, melted and cast down into this love, speaks freely and respectfully to God as though to one's own father" (9.18).⁹³ Prayers were to be *frequent* and *brief*, because distractions intrude if prayer is wordy (9.36).⁹⁴

In *Conference 10*, we read that Germanus asks for "a formula which will enable us to think of God and to hold incessantly to that thought so that, as we keep it in view, we may have something to return to immediately whenever we find that we have somehow slipped away from it. It will be there for us to take up once more without wasting time in searches or in painful detours" (10.8).⁹⁵ In reply, Abba Isaac gives a formula, saying: "Every monk who wants to think continuously about God should get accustomed to meditating endlessly on it and banishing all other thoughts for its sake." He goes on to say that "this is something which has been handed on to us by some of the oldest of the fathers".⁹⁶

He then gives the teaching: "Cling totally to this formula for piety: *'Come to my help, O God; Lord, hurry to my rescue'*" (Ps 69:2 LXX). He adds that this verse "carries within it all the feelings of which human nature is capable" (10.10).⁹⁷ He later advises that "the thought of this verse should be turning unceasingly in your heart. Never cease to recite it in whatever task or service or journey you find yourself . . . a formula of salvation for you . . . (it) will lead you on to the contemplation of the unseen and the heavenly and to that fiery urgency of prayer, which is indescribable and which is experienced by very few" (10.10). In addition, he states: "The soul must fiercely grab onto this formula so that after saying it over and over again, after meditating upon it without pause, it has the strength to reject and to refuse all the abundant riches of thought" (10.11).⁹⁸ This prayer "is a fiery outbreak, an indescribable exaltation, an insatiable thrust of the soul. Free of what is sensed and seen, ineffable in its groans and sighs, the soul pours itself out to God" (10.11).⁹⁹ Constant attention and firm concentration is required.¹⁰⁰ This gives stability to the soul which cannot be obtained except by effort.¹⁰¹

The prayer formula described by Cassian represented an early tradition of prayer for help and protection, but within monasticism it later became eclipsed by the *Kyrie eleison* style of prayer such as the Jesus Prayer, particularly after the fourth century.¹⁰² In this latter approach confession of sin and compunction were seen as the starting point of asceticism. *Penthos* (compunction) was seen as the most effective means to continual prayer and the one least likely to produce illusion.¹⁰³

John Chrysostom (c.347–407) also advocated the use of frequent, short prayers of choice. Prayer formulas after his time began to be stereotyped and immutable.[104]

Diadochus of Photike

Diadochus of Photike (born c.400) in the mid-fifth century considered the habitual thought or memory of God and of the Lord Jesus as indicative of perfection.[105] He is the first writer to refer explicitly to the remembrance of the Name of Jesus, although he does not offer an exact form for the invocation.[106] He wrote:

> If then a man begins to make progress in keeping the commandments and calls ceaselessly upon the Lord Jesus, the fire of God's grace spreads even to the heart's more outward organs of perception, consciously burning up the tares in the field of the soul.[107]

As noted by Metropolitan Kallistos Ware, Diadochus made a very important contribution to the development of the Jesus Prayer by linking the repeated invocation of the Name of Jesus to entry into the inner stillness of *hesychia*.[108] He recognized that in reaching towards the prayer of inner silence it was necessary to deal with the incessant activity of the mind. Hence:

> When we have blocked all its outlets by means of the remembrance of God, the intellect requires of us imperatively some task which will satisfy its need for activity. For the complete fulfillment of its purpose we should give it nothing but the prayer "Lord Jesus" . . . Let the intellect continually concentrate on these words within its inner shrine with such intensity that it is not turned aside to any mental images.[109]

Hausherr considered that the essence of the Jesus Prayer comprises "a request for mercy together with the name or title of the Saviour that implies an act of faith in him as Messiah, as Son of God, as God himself".[110] He cited evidence that Dorotheus of Gaza in the first half of the sixth century taught the Jesus Prayer in its full form to his disciple Dosithy.[111] The full text of the Jesus Prayer is mentioned in the sixth or seventh century in *The Life of Abba Philimon*, an Egyptian hermit.[112] When asked what to do to avoid distraction, Philimon replied: "Keep watch in your heart; and with watchfulness say in your mind with awe and trembling: 'Lord Jesus Christ, have mercy upon me.'"[113] In another place he wrote: "Lord, Jesus Christ, Son of God, have mercy on me."[114]

St John of the Ladder

John Climacus (570–649), abbot of St Catherine's monastery on Mount Sinai and author of *The Ladder of Divine Ascent*, emphasized the invocation of the Name of Jesus.[115] In Step 21 of *The Ladder* he wrote: "Flog your enemies with the name of Jesus, since there is no stronger weapon in heaven or on earth."[116] In Step 27 he stated: "Let the remembrance of Jesus be present with your every breath. Then indeed you will appreciate the value of stillness."[117] In Step 28 he taught that engaging in wordy prayers causes distraction. Instead, brevity makes for concentration.[118] He advised: "Make the effort to raise up, or rather, to enclose your mind within the words of your prayer . . . "[119]

The writings of Pseudo-Hesychios (probably eighth- or ninth-century), which were later than those of Climacus, use the expression "Prayer of Jesus" (*Iesou evchē*) and the connection of the prayer with breathing:[120] "Truly blessed is the man whose mind and heart are as closely attached to the Jesus Prayer and the ceaseless invocation of his Name as air to the body or flame to the wax."[121] This author represents a further trend toward uniformity in the prayer formula.

Mount Athos and the Slavic lands

The tradition of hesychasm, which flourished on Mount Athos in the fourteenth century, has been discussed in chapter 3. Its practice of inner silence involves a positive attitude of attentive alertness, vigilance and listening.[122] The Jesus Prayer was a central element in this mystical tradition.[123] During this period it became more established as a fixed formula. It also became associated with certain psychophysical techniques.[124] The hesychast sought pure prayer, encountering God within the heart.[125]

Gregory of Sinai (1255–1346) learned of the Jesus Prayer while living in Crete and later went to Mount Athos, where he instructed the monks there in its practice. He later travelled again and settled near Bulgaria. Through his influence hesychasm and the practice of the Jesus Prayer spread throughout the Slavic countries.[126]

Nikiphoros (c.1300), an Italian who became a monk on Mount Athos, in his work *On Guarding the Heart* stressed the need for instruction by an experienced spiritual teacher in order to practise prayer and overcome spiritual obstacles.[127] He wrote about some of the psychophysical practices of hesychasm, connecting the Jesus Prayer with breathing and postural techniques. He described a method of concentrating the mind on the inhaled breath and descending with it into the heart, the Jesus Prayer being repeated unceasingly. As will be discussed in chapter 5, the psychophysical practices of hesychasm bear similarities to some of the practices of yoga and Islamic Sufism.[128]

Gregory Palamas (1296–1359) was a monk on Mount Athos and later Archbishop of Thessalonica. In the controversy instigated by Barlaam, he defended techniques (such as those involving breathing and posture associated with the Jesus Prayer) as practical ways for beginners to avoid distraction and the wandering of the mind. Such methods were not merely mechanical means to obtain grace.[129] The divine illumination experienced in prayer was not simply intellectual but involved the whole person, including the body.

The practice of the Jesus Prayer also spread in Russia, promoted by such spiritual luminaries as Nil Sorsky in the fifteenth century and Dimitri of Rostov in the seventeenth century.[130] In the eighteenth century Makarios of Corinth (1731–1805) and Nikodemos the Hagiorite (1748–1809) published *The Philokalia*, an anthology of patristic texts by authors from the fourth to the fifteenth centuries. The publication of this text revived hesychasm in nineteenth-century Greece and Russia.

In 1793, Paisius Velichkovsky (1722–94) published a Slavonic edition, entitled *Dobrotolubiye*.[131] The practice of the Jesus Prayer flourished in nineteenth-century Russia, assisted by the Elders at Optino and the great Seraphim of Sarov (1759–1833). Other important teachers were Ignatius Brianchaninov (1807–67) and Theophan the Recluse (1815–94). During this period an anonymously authored work known as *The Way of the Pilgrim* appeared, describing the discovery of the Jesus Prayer by a Russian peasant in search of a way to "pray without ceasing". This work, which may not be autobiographical, greatly popularized the practice of the prayer.[132] During the twentieth century, the practice of the Jesus Prayer spread beyond the boundaries of Eastern Orthodoxy and indeed its original monastic setting and became more widely known to people of other Christian denominations.

While very prevalent in groups and individuals affiliated to the Orthodox Church, it has become more widely practised outside such groups, even sometimes being detached from the sacramental and liturgical life of the Church.[133] Personal guidance by a spiritual father or teacher in the practice of the prayer has also become less prevalent.

The Holy Name in the West

Rama Coomaraswamy has documented extensive devotion to the Holy Name of Jesus in the Western Church. He wrote a book in the hope of providing a theological basis for its use as "a prayer eminently suitable to contemporary man and the present times".[134] He wrote of its scriptural basis and the power of the Name and reflected on the theological significance of the invocation of the Name. Much of his book comprises sermons and teachings from various illustrious saints of the Church in the West who extolled devotion to the Holy Name of Jesus. These include Bernadine of Siena, Bonaventure, Thomas Aquinas, Bernard of

Clairvaux, Anthony of Padua, Peter Canisius and Ignatius Loyola, who made the Name and its symbolic form "IHS" the seal of the Jesuit Order.

Coomaraswamy advocated that this form of the prayer should be practised within a traditional framework and with a spiritual director familiar with the Way of the Name.

The Marian rosary

Given the obvious widespread devotion to the Holy Name of Jesus, it seems puzzling that unlike the Marian rosary, something akin to the Jesus Prayer did not become a continuing universal form of popular piety and spiritual practice in the West. There are some similarities between the Marian rosary and the Jesus Prayer, in so far as both involve repetitive invocations. Moreover, it is usually prayed with the assistance of beads to promote focused concentration. The rosary beads thus have some resemblance to the prayer rope commonly used with the Jesus Prayer. Despite these technical similarities, the rosary is quite different to the Jesus Prayer in both its history and its content. Unlike the Jesus Prayer, it is a devotion that evolved in the Middle Ages in the West.[135] Its central invocation is: "Hail Mary, full of grace, the Lord is with you", a prayer derived from the angelic salutation of Mary in the New Testament (Luke 1:28) and Elizabeth's greeting: "Blessed are you among women, and blessed is the fruit of your womb" (Luke 1:42). This basic form of the prayer emerged in the twelfth century. During the thirteenth and fourteenth centuries, the name "Jesus" was appended to the prayer, and in the sixteenth century the phrase "Holy Mary, Mother of God, pray for us sinners now and at the hour of our death" was added.[136]

The "Hail Marys" are prayed in groups of ten ("decades") represented by ten beads and each group is separated by a single bead representing the "Our Father". A set of rosary beads includes five decades. The practice is for each set of five decades to be designated as a "Mystery" consisting of specific themes and events in the life of Jesus. They are classified as Joyful Mysteries, Sorrowful Mysteries and Glorious Mysteries, with the more recent Mysteries of Light being added by Pope John Paul II in 2002. While reciting the invocations to Mary counted with the beads, the practice is to simultaneously reflect on the appropriate scriptural events. Hence by its combination of invocations and imaginative reflections the Marian rosary uses a method of prayer which differs significantly from the Jesus Prayer.

The development of the rosary arose out of the practice of recitations of the 150 Psalms of the Old Testament. In "Marian Psalters", antiphons which preceded each Psalm came to be replaced by short verses interpreting each Psalm as a reference to Christ or Mary.

Gradually the prayers were shortened and now consisted of the antiphons alone and either Our Fathers or Hail Marys. The antiphons became replaced by paraphrases or verses in praise of Mary. At that stage, there was no connected narrative theme and, as a result, much difficulty in remembering the verses. This problem was remedied by the development of "Life of Christ" meditations in which scenes from the life of Jesus were inserted into the praises of Mary. As result of this narrative form, the attention of the person praying the rosary could be focused on the particular theme applicable to each decade as it was being recited. This crucial transition to a "Life of Christ Rosary" led to the development of the characteristic structure of the modern rosary. The further additions of the Creed and the Gloria became a means of summarizing doctrines of the Faith. The rosary thereby served to reinforce orthodoxy and combat heresy as well as providing a means of catechizing the unlettered.[137]

CHAPTER 5

The Indian Connection: Yoga, Mantras and Meditation

Wise men from the East came to Jerusalem, asking, "Where is the child who has been born king of the Jews? For we observed his star at its rising, and have come to pay him homage."
Matthew 2:1–2

At this stage in our journey we turn further to the East, beyond the boundaries of Christianity. Although non-Christian religions and traditions are peripheral matters in relation to the Jesus Prayer, there are reasons for us to consider such influences. The Indian traditions of yoga and Meditation, in particular, are relevant for several reasons. Firstly, it has been claimed that some of the psychophysical hesychastic practices were derived from Hindu yoga via Sufism, a mystical tradition within Islam. In addition, there is a clear connection between Indian mantra Meditation practices and the development of the system of Christian Meditation advocated by a Benedictine monk, John Main. Finally, Eastern religions and Meditation practices have become popular in the West and have attracted many Christians. Accordingly, this phenomenon makes it desirable to compare the Jesus Prayer with those traditions. I believe that by doing so it will become apparent to Christians that there is no reason for them to look beyond their own faith tradition to fulfil their spiritual needs and to find a sure path to their heart's desire through the Jesus Prayer.

Yoga

Although I make no attempt in this chapter to provide more than a brief overview of yoga and Hindu Meditation, what follows is sufficient for our purposes in understanding the relevance of this tradition to Christian prayer and Meditation. Hinduism developed six schools of thought considered to be ways of salvation. One of these is the system of yoga. Having arisen in ancient times, yoga in a broad sense has been part of the teaching of every Indian sect.[138] Yoga is much more than just a metaphysical school of thought as its practices encompass moral rules, psychophysical practices including postures and breathing techniques, and methods of Meditation. Yoga has been described as a practical system of spirituality, which, despite not being a religion as such, can be practised within any religion.[139]

The classic text of the School of Yoga is the *Yoga Sutras* of Patañjali, a teacher who was thought to have lived in the second century BC. The system outlined by Patañjali introduces one of the oldest statements of the structure of theistic Meditation.[140] The *Yoga Sutras* state that the highest spiritual state, known as *samādhi*, can be achieved by self-surrender to the Lord ("Īśvara").[141] However, Īśvara does not meet all the attributes of God as Creator in the Christian understanding. The *Yoga Sutras* define Īśvara as: "a distinct person/spirit untouched by the impact of life's afflictions, actions and the residual fruits of actions".[142] They also state that:

> In Him the source of omniscience is without limit.[143]
>
> Transcending time, He is the teacher even of the Ancients.[144]
>
> He is manifested verbally as the mantra "OM".[145]
>
> Constant repetition (*japah*) and meditation (*bhāvanam*) on its meaning[146] results in the removal of obstacles and consciousness turning inward.[147]

Arthur L. Basham has summarized the eight stages in the system of yoga as follows:

1. Self-control (*yama*), the practice of the five moral rules: non-violence, truthfulness, non-stealing, chastity, and the avoidance of greed;
2. Observance (*niyama*), the regular and complete observance of five further moral rules, some of them rather overlapping with those in the category of self-control: purity, contentment, austerity, study of the Vedas and devotion to God;
3. Posture (āsana), sitting in certain postures, difficult without practice, which are thought to be essential to Meditation. The most famous of these is *padmāsana*, the "Lotus Posture", in which the feet are placed on the opposite thighs, and in which gods and sages are commonly depicted;
4. Control of the Breath (*prāṇāyāma*), whereby the breath is held and controlled, and the respiration forced into unusual rhythms, which are believed to be of great physical and spiritual value;
5. Restraint (*pratyāhāra*), whereby the sense organs are trained to take no note of their perceptions;
6. Steadying the Mind (*dhāraṇā*), by concentration on a single object, such as the tip of the nose, the navel, an icon, or a sacred symbol;
7. Meditation (*dhyāna*), when the object of concentration fills the whole mind;
8. Deep Meditation (*samādhi*), when the whole personality is temporarily dissolved.[148]

The essence of yoga is to control the fluctuations of the mind. The *Yoga Sutras* define it as "the inhibition of the mind's modifications".[149] Accordingly, all of the components of the path of yoga are directed towards this goal of complete cessation of fluctuating thought.

The moral principles of *yama* and *niyama* are considered to be preliminary aspects of the practice of yoga. The yogic āsanas are described in the *Yoga Sutras* as postures which are characterized by steadiness (*sthiram*) and ease (*sukham*).[150] These consist of a wide range of physical manoeuvres involving stretching and compression of various limbs and parts of the body, culminating in periods of static maintenance in particular postures. These postures, which relieve physical stiffness and tension, are aimed at bringing relaxation, flexibility, balance, optimal physiological functioning and health for the body as well as being conducive to calmness of mind.

There are also a range of physical practices (*kriyās*) aimed at personal hygiene and optimizing health. Particular āsanas have attracted names such as the bow posture, the cobra posture, the tree posture, etc. because of their particular spatial configurations. The seated Lotus Pose (*padmāsana*) is one of the classic poses suited for Meditation. Nonetheless, for most people the Easy Pose (*sukhāsana*) is the most convenient to practice.[151] It is conducive to both comfort and steadiness and can be maintained for a significant period of time. It involves sitting cross legged on a mat or carpet on the floor, or sitting on a cushion or low stool, with the spine held up straight and the hands resting with palms downward on each knee. With eyes closed, the meditator can enter into a relaxed and composed mental state "like patience on a monument smiling at grief".[152]

The practices of *prāṇāyāma* involve the conscious control of the breath. They range from the simple practice of equalizing the time of inhaling and exhaling to much more complex breathing patterns. These latter practices involve producing specific time ratios for the various components of the breathing process. The relative time spent on each of the phases—inhalation; holding the breath after inhaling; exhalation; and holding the breath on exhalation—can be varied according to particular ratios. These practices are said to have specific psychic and physiological effects. Although *prāṇāyāma* refers to breathing practices, they are viewed as exerting their effects by regulating, conserving and controlling energy levels. Whatever the reality in that regard, it is consistent with the widely recognized close linkage between a person's breathing patterns and their mental state.

Beginning with the process of *pratyāhāra*, involving control of the senses and directing them inwards, the practice of yoga then progresses from concentration (*dhāraṇā*) to Meditation (*dhyāna*) and then to *samādhi*. *Samādhi* occurs when self-awareness falls away and one's consciousness is completely absorbed by the object of Meditation. This is reminiscent of the saying attributed to Antony of Egypt, that in perfect prayer a person no longer perceives himself praying.

Patañjali's *Yoga Sutras* also refer to the acquisition of higher psychic powers called *siddhis* which arise with progress on the path of yoga.[153] These consist of various paranormal phenomena such as clairvoyance and levitation. It should be noted that Patañjali warned that such powers are obstacles on the spiritual path and are to be disregarded.[154] They produce many temptations and distractions, resulting in falls because they turn the mind outward and away from progressing deeper into the truth. This is reminiscent of Christian beliefs about the fall of Satan through pride. Yogis are also tempted to try to usurp higher powers for themselves, with demonic consequences. This has been exemplified in modern times by numerous cases of so-called gurus being revealed as malevolent and narcissistic cult leaders, wreaking psychological and spiritual devastation on their hapless followers.

Mantras

It is necessary to consider the nature of the mantra tradition in Hinduism to understand the debate about mantra-like features of Christian prayer and Meditation. Due to their great diversity, it is difficult to provide a general definition of "mantra". Gonda considered that our modern languages do not possess a single term that would cover what Indians understand as mantra.[155] The *Australian Concise Oxford Dictionary* defines it as:

> 1 a word or sound repeated to aid concentration in meditation, originally in Hinduism and Buddhism. 2 a Vedic hymn. 3 a statement or slogan repeated frequently.[156]

The original meaning of the word, which relates to Hindu and Buddhist practices, has broadened subsequently and passed into modern colloquial usage to refer to any repetitive words or phrases, without any necessary religious connotations.

In India, all sound is perceived as being divine in origin and bearing the power of the sacred.[157] In Hinduism the sacred syllable "OM" is seen as the supreme creative word from which all other sounds have arisen, and it is therefore seen as the supreme root mantra from which all others arose. The Vedic seers were believed to have "heard" divine mantras super-sensuously as revelations of eternal truth.

By concentrating upon such mantras a devotee could purportedly purify his or her consciousness. Mantras in the Ṛg Veda period were essential for the performance of rituals. They were used to invoke and praise the gods, dedicate oblations, express the meaning and function of rituals and avert evil influences.[158] Although not prayers as such, mantras were sometimes used as prayers.[159] They were seen to have power, representing the truth and order at the centre of the universe. When spoken, a mantra released power that could be used for good or ill and required correct pronunciation in ritual by a priest.[160] Mantras were seen as part of the revelation of truth, and through their ongoing repetition cosmic truth and order were believed to be manifested and preserved.

Following the Vedic period the highest and most effective mantras were not the loudest ones but the more silent, subtle and purely mental utterances.[161] In later developments, mantras became keys to Meditation, seen as maintaining contact with the divine. They could also be chanted in a "magical" fashion to achieve worldly goals. During the time of the Upanishads the emphasis shifted to the use of mantras given by a teacher or *guru* to the student to reveal knowledge with the redemptive goal of final spiritual release (*mokṣa*).[162] During the medieval period there were yoga traditions using sound vibrations as the basis for Meditational techniques. They recognized that mantras produced vibrations affecting a person's psychophysical state, involving states of consciousness and inner feelings.[163] In Hinduism, the repeated chanting of mantras, a practice known as *japa*, is believed to remove all impurities and lead to final release.[164]

Patañjali taught that Īśvara is embodied in the mantra "OM" which is produced by his will. Reciting the mantra could reveal the divine consciousness and release the power of the deity. He advocated constant repetition and Meditation on its meaning as the most effective means of overcoming the distracted mind. He stipulated that the repetitions were not to be merely mechanical, but Meditation on the significance of the mantra was needed to establish contact with the deity.[165] The result of such complete self-surrender was considered to be a face-to-face encounter with God.

The theistic traditions of the worship of God as Śiva or Viṣṇu also advocated Meditation on mantras to produce an encounter with God. Having both meaning and power, mantras were seen as having a sacramental type of function. From the sixth century onwards, Tantrism became a pan-Indian tradition. Tantric mantras aimed to annihilate all distinctions and affirm the worshipper's identity with the divine. A unique feature of Tantrism was its teaching about the Great Goddess whose power (Śakti) was said to sustain the universe. The Tantric tradition included sometimes partial or mutilated words, or bizarre and unintelligible phonemes known as *dhāraṇīs* for chanting in Meditation.[166] Mantras and *dhāraṇīs* were considered vehicles of salvation and had to be specially received from the mouth of a guru.[167]

From the Vedic period onwards, mantras developed different characteristics from those of ordinary language, with their phonetic structures becoming more important than their obvious meaning, if any. Instead of being used as language they performed direct actions, usually ritualistic, psychological or mystical. From the Vedic to the Tantric period mantras tended to become more repetitive and increasingly poorer in linguistic content and phonetic variety, thus tending toward silence.[168]

Meditation

Meditation in one form or another has been practised in many cultures and in many religious traditions. It has been central to the contemplative traditions in all the great religions. A precise definition is difficult, because Meditation can take many forms, and it therefore encompasses a wide range of phenomena. Shapiro et al. have suggested:

> Meditation can be defined as a family of practices that train attention and awareness, usually with the aim of fostering psychological and spiritual well-being and maturity. Meditation does this by training and bringing mental processes under greater voluntary control and directing them in beneficial ways.[169]

The two very common forms of Meditation consist of practices of either concentration or awareness. These contrasting approaches have been compared to the difference between a restrictive technique, akin to a zoom lens focusing on a specific object within a field, and an expansive, opening-up technique like a wide-angle lens focusing on the whole field.[170]

Concentrative Meditation involves awareness focused upon a single stimulus such as a mantra or the breathing rhythm. The description of Meditation in the *Yoga Sutras* is of the concentrative type. Transcendental Meditation (TM) is probably the most commonly practised contemporary form of such mantra Meditation. The claim that the Jesus Prayer is a form of mantra Meditation is discussed further in chapter 12. John Main taught Christian Meditation as a mantra-based method.

Those types of Meditation that employ awareness instead of concentration, such as Insight or "Mindfulness" Meditation, involve a state of active passivity in which the meditator

> purposefully and non-judgementally pays attention to the present moment, attending to the multitude of sights, sounds, sensations, feelings, and thoughts that simultaneously present themselves to his or her awareness in each moment. His or her focus is on the process, or flow of psychic content, rather than on the content itself.[171]

Another variety of Meditation involves the experience of what can be termed "thoughtless awareness". In contrast to concentrative and other awareness systems of Meditation, the method of Centering Prayer advocated by Thomas Keating involves the conscious surrender or letting go of thoughts.[172] It is widely claimed that the practice of Meditation promotes physical, psychological and spiritual wellbeing. There have been many research studies suggesting beneficial effects although many of them have been limited by less than adequate methodologies.

In Mindfulness Meditation the subject becomes the object of awareness. In this meditation a dis-identification of the observing self from the ego occurs. The meditator maintains awareness of the flow of experience rather than the contents, and a split occurs in which the observing self sees itself as separate from the contents of awareness. There is a heightened receptivity of perceptions. Derived from the Buddhist tradition but adapted as a secular practice, it has become a popular component of psychological therapies. Some studies have suggested that Mindfulness can help with treatment of various conditions such as anxiety, drug addictions, depression, chronic pain problems, hypertension and insomnia.[173]

Meditation can be practised as a purely psychological process without any religious goal. Nevertheless, the widespread practice of Meditation in religious traditions highlights the importance of such practices for those pursuing the spiritual path. Psychologically a meditator can gain greater self-knowledge, with insight into his or her mental functioning. The repeated focusing of attention is inevitably met with distracting and intrusive thoughts, images or feelings. Disturbing or unpleasant memories and emotions that have hitherto been unconscious or repressed often surface into conscious awareness. This phenomenon has sometimes been referred to by psychologists as "unstressing". Such anxiety-laden material usually dissipates and is followed by a feeling of relaxation and calmness. In mantra Meditation, the flow of thoughts and distractions gradually diminishes and leads to a state of "no thought".

Goleman and Davidson have noted the increased scientific interest in Meditation since the early research studies in the 1970s. Over the past decade there has been a massive increase in the number of scientific articles on the topic.[174] Notwithstanding the proliferation of such studies, many of them fail to meet the highest standards of scientific research methodology. Despite these caveats there is emerging evidence that Meditation practices can produce significant changes in brain functioning. In their review of the research data, Goleman and Davidson have found evidence of changes in brain circuitry arising from Meditation practices, in processes such as retraining attention or cultivating compassion and empathy. They considered that Meditation practices show promise of having beneficial therapeutic effects on anxiety, depression, pain and stress. They suggest that through neuroplasticity mechanisms in the brain, increasing amounts of Meditation practice may result in temporary changes developing into enduring traits. Of particular interest is their report of findings that experienced Tibetan yogis exhibited highly elevated levels of gamma brainwave oscillations. The high-frequency gamma waves reflect synchronous activity in differing brain regions such as that which occurs during moments of insight.[175]

While for most people the experience of Meditation is calming, refreshing and therapeutic, occasionally there are adverse effects. There have been reported cases of acute, usually brief, psychotic states precipitated by Meditation.[176] Half of such patients had a psychiatric history, especially a history of psychotic symptoms. Other vulnerability factors include sleep deprivation, and physical exhaustion caused by fasting. There have been reports of Transcendental Meditation producing adverse reactions including depression, suicidal impulses, agitation and restlessness. More subtle adverse effects may simply result in people discontinuing the practice of TM.[177] On the other hand, Meditation practices have often been beneficial for people with psychiatric problems. Meditation is obviously not suitable for everyone.

East meets West

An early attempt to relate yoga to Christian life was made by Benedictine monk J-M. Déchanet in his book *Christian Yoga*, first published in 1960.[178] He sought to utilize the yoga postures to make his body "a fitter instrument for contemplation".[179] Nevertheless he wrote that he felt the need to be careful that the higher meditative practices should not turn him towards the Absolute and "Ungraspable" of Hinduism but towards the living God of Abraham, Isaac, and Jacob. As a Christian he realized that no methodology would unite him with God and that "every technique is subordinated to the initiative coming from God".[180]

He considered that it was not a question of turning a given form of yoga into something Christian, but of bringing into the service of the Christian life benefits from the yoga practices.[181] There should be no syncretism but only the introduction of methods to assist the Christian path. He envisaged the techniques of yoga creating optimal conditions for being attentive to God. He gave guidance on practising the physical elements of yoga. He accepted the higher meditative aspects at the level of technique or skill while rejecting elements of Hindu philosophy and theology incompatible with Christian doctrine.[182]

More recently, an Indian Christian author, J. Clement Vaz, advocated a program of Christian prayer and Meditation utilizing the methodology of yoga, which he considered to be of potential value for Christian spiritual life. He advocated yoga as a means of enhancing Christian prayer, especially the profound silence leading to the experience of God.[183] His adaptation of classical yoga to Christian spirituality raises for the Church the issue of the appropriate parameters of incorporating practices from non-Christian sources. The Christian message being universal, it need not be expressed only in terms applicable to one specific culture, such as that of the Greco-Roman world. It must instead develop ways of being manifested in many different societies and cultures. This involves some incorporation of indigenous customs and traditions into its religious practices. Therefore it might be argued that appropriate forms of yoga can have a legitimate role within the life of the Church in India.

Thomas Ryan argued that Meditation and yoga can enrich Christian spiritual practice. He recognized that Meditation in all religious traditions is a search for the God within and "part of the universal spiritual culture of humankind".[184] He acknowledged that when practised outside the context of Christian faith, it often amounts to Pelagianism; an attempt to achieve salvation through human effort alone despite the fact that salvation is the divine work of God in Christ.[185] He advocated the use of a mantra to dispose oneself to contemplative prayer.[186] He noted that the mantra is a tool which helps to alter consciousness by breaking down the ordinary connection between speech and thought, such that prayer is lifted up beyond the limits of language and conceptual thought. In his view, the lack of images and mental associations attached to the mantra assists the movement towards God in faith.[187] Through self-surrender the Christian meditator enters into the prayer of Christ.

Ryan also endorsed the value of the physical practices of yoga. He considered that they can serve as preparation for Meditation. He viewed the yogic disciplines as being able to help people become disposed to receive the graces of contemplation. He recognized the essential role of synergy in the spiritual path, in which both human and divine aspects combine and work together in freedom.[188] The human contribution is to make ourselves open and receptive to God's actions.

Thomas Matus, a Camaldolese Benedictine monk, had come to the Catholic faith in his adult life after previous contact with Hindu and Buddhist spiritual disciplines. He wrote that he was led through his practice of yoga meditation to discover Jesus as not only one of many "masters", or even the greatest of *gurus*, but as "the Son of God, 'light from light, true God from true God'".[189] He then asked himself what meaning yoga could have for a person whose spiritual identity was defined by belonging to Christ and the Church. He noted that many questioned whether the practice of yoga could lead to an experience which is truly Christian.[190] He considered that the Christian use of yoga means that faith in Jesus penetrates the yogic practice and is its starting point and motivation. Its value depends on integrating personal faith with the yoga practice.[191]

Matus referred to Christian yoga as "the yoga of Christ".[192] This is the yoga of the cross and resurrection. In yoga terminology, Meditation on Christ is transient; it is *dhāraṇā*. When constant, it is *dhyāna*, communion with His person; and Christian *samādhi* is being assimilated into Christ, expressed in a life of love and renunciation of self. The ultimate *mantra*, of infinite "vibration", is the Name of Jesus, the only name "by which we must be saved" (Acts 4:12).

Indian Jesuit Anthony de Mello (1931–87) embraced both Eastern and Western traditions in his career as a retreat director, spiritual teacher and author. A prolific storyteller, he drew upon the wisdom teachings of various traditions to help stimulate spiritual awakening and understanding in his listeners. His stories served as modern parables to engage a deeper level than the literalism of the discursive mind. He taught various practices derived from Eastern religious traditions. For example, he taught mindful awareness focusing on bodily sensations, breathing rhythms, stillness, sounds and silence.[193] He realized that such exercises do not appear to be meditation or prayer in the traditional sense of speaking with God. He saw contemplation as communication with God with minimal or no use of words, images, or concepts. He made the important observation that the mystics teach us that we are endowed with a mystical mind and heart, a faculty that makes it possible to know God directly. This appears consistent with the Eastern Orthodox teachings of John Romanides about the *nous* as discussed previously in chapter 3. In most of us this mystical heart is dormant and undeveloped.[194] Its awakening involves bypassing the thoughts, words, and images that stand between us and God. The spiritual contemplative practices which Anthony de Mello recommended were aimed at assisting this process.[195] He nonetheless displayed a strong Ignatian influence from his Jesuit background by advocating imagination and sensory images in many of the practices that he recommended.

De Mello noted that the practice of *lectio divina* "offers the head some participation in prayer and thus keeps it from being distracted. At the same time, it gently takes the prayer away from discourse and reflection into simplicity and affectivity."[196] He also pointed out that it is erroneous to consider vocal prayer with a set form of words as inferior to mental prayer. Praying verbally is much more likely to lead into contemplation than praying with thoughts. He noted the teaching of John Climacus to recite a prayer formula with perfect attention to both the words of the prayer and to the Person to whom the prayer is addressed.[197]

In his discussion of the Jesus Prayer, de Mello noted that the repetition of the name gets into the depths of one's being and transforms one's heart and mind. He also made the important observation that the name of Jesus is no more than a means of leading us to Jesus himself and is worthless if it does not have that effect.[198] In contrast to the Eastern Orthodox teachers, however, he recommended the more questionable practice of using imagery, such as imagining Jesus saying words to us. This suggestion goes further than the practice suggested by Teresa of Avila of imagining Jesus standing before us and looking humbly and lovingly at us, a practice not intended to promote imagery. It is a practice to help focus on the divine presence and the actions of Jesus which are occurring in the present reality. Hence it is "worship in spirit and in truth", rather than something derived from our own fantasies.[199]

In a comprehensive analysis, Kallistos Ware discussed the physical techniques proposed by the fourteenth-century hesychasts and acknowledged that they suggest obvious parallels with the practices of yoga and Sufi Islam.[200] In reviewing the history of the Jesus Prayer, he noted that the early writers gave no indication of employing a physical technique in the prayer. Statements such as those of John Climacus (seventh century), "Let the remembrance of Jesus be united with your breathing", could indicate a physical method associated with breathing, but equally they could be simply metaphorical, suggesting that prayer should be as constant and spontaneous as our breathing.

He noted that the Coptic material from around the seventh or eighth centuries seemed to suggest a definite connection between the breathing rhythm and the invocation of Jesus. It affirmed a central feature advocated by the hesychasts that Jesus be invoked with every breath.[201] He noted further that the next textual evidence, dated to around the late thirteenth century, comprised two texts; the first by Nikiphoros on watchfulness and the guarding of the heart, and the second by Pseudo-Simeon on the Three Methods of Prayer. The next mention of a physical technique is by Gregory of Sinai in the fourteenth century. Later in the same century there is a work by Kallistos and Ignatios Xanthopoulos. These authors describe the technique much criticized by Barlaam, advocating three main features: a particular bodily posture; a controlled breathing rhythm; and an inner quest to find the place of the heart.

Around these centuries the introduction of notable changes is recorded. Firstly, in contrast to the traditional Christian practice of standing for prayer, a significant innovation occurs with the recommended posture being to sit while saying the Jesus Prayer. In his writings on the patristic traditions of prayer, Gabriel Bunge noted the general custom was to stand while praying, a biblical and apostolic tradition which the early Church continued.[202]

A second important development occurred around control of the breath. While Nikiphoros and Pseudo-Simeon suggested it should be preliminary to the prayer, Gregory of Sinai and the Xanthopouloi indicated that it was to be simultaneous with the prayer and directly combined with the actual invocation. The act of breathing and the prayer were thereby combined to produce the unceasing remembrance of God.[203]

The third feature was the inner quest for the place of the heart. Ware emphasized that the heart was understood in the biblical sense as being the centre of the whole human person, and that it "has a connotation both physical and spiritual, both literal and symbolic". It was both a bodily organ and the spiritual centre of a person.[204] Therefore the hesychasts advised that through concentrating on the physical heart we are able to enter our deepest centre, the meeting point between the soul and God. These observations raise the question of whether these changes came about through contact with external influences such as yoga or Sufism.

Ware observed that none of the authorities which he cited stated that the physical method was indispensable, compulsory or that it constituted the essence of inner prayer.[205] Moreover, according to Gregory Palamas the physical methods were not for the experienced hesychasts but for beginners. They were seen as a useful aid for some but optional. Invoking the name of Jesus with concentration and faith was the essence of the prayer whereas the manner of seating, breathing and fixing attention was purely secondary.

In a lecture to the Guild of Pastoral Psychology, London in 1957, Metropolitan Anthony Bloom (1914–2003), himself a medical doctor, spoke about the psychophysical ("somatopsychic") techniques which in the hesychast tradition have been found to aid spiritual attainment. Consistent with the patristic teachings mentioned in chapter 3 about the reciprocal interaction of soul and body, Bloom noted that "every psychic activity carries its somatic repercussion and inversely, that attitudes and movements of the body may favour, even provoke, mental states. The body, perceptibly or imperceptibly, takes part in every movement of the soul—whether of feeling, of abstract thought, of volition, or even of transcendent experience."[206] He explained that when a predominant thought or sentiment occurs, a focus of concentration arises and defines itself with certain somatopsychic traits. He identified the following centres which have been specified by Orthodox ascetics:

- *Cranial Cerebro-Frontal Centre* in the interciliary region (between the eyebrows) which is associated with abstract, purely intellectual thought.
- *Bucco Laryngeal Centre* focused around the mouth, larynx and throat region associated with verbal thought combined with an emotional charge. This is the commonest form of thought expressed in conversation and in the first verbal stages of prayer.
- *Pectoral Centre* in the upper medial section of the chest with thought progressing towards the centre of unification and concentration. This is associated with silent prayer.

- *Cardiac Centre* situated on the upper section of the heart which is the physical locus of perfect attention. At this level thought is concentrated with complete cohesion sufficient to repel all alien emotion.[207]

This latter form of concentration in the secular realm can be caused by any powerful emotion such as joy or sorrow, and in the spiritual realm it is associated with encounter with the Divine Presence of the Living God. In this state,

> the intelligence persists without fatigue in prayer or meditation. Free of all struggle, of all incertitude, and of all anxiety, it acquires a lucidity, a vigilance, a power, a brilliance hitherto unknown to it. This state will only cease when the reviving grace of the Holy Spirit suspends its action.[208]

Here sentiment is vital, pure, and devoid of all passion. This noetic state is fully conscious and free. Bloom stated that techniques which help to detect and localize this point artificially are not in themselves designed to produce prayer but to teach the novice where this optimum centre of attention is so that at the appropriate time they may recognize it as a point of origin for their prayer. He also noted that attention may be fixed on this Heart Centre quite apart from prayer. Prayer, however, starts with an act of faith, is not dependent upon artificial methods and it constitutes a free self-gift from both the person praying and God.

Bloom taught that focusing attention below the heart region is to be avoided as it engenders other sensations which can arouse uncontrollable desires and passions. Not surprisingly, he pointed out that the use of these physical techniques absolutely requires the direction of a suitably experienced Master. He explained that these techniques do not constitute contemplative prayer but rather a preparatory form for such prayer to occur, after which spiritual work begins. Potential dangers of the physical methods have been emphasized by other modern Orthodox authorities, who insist that they should only be used under the strict guidance of an experienced spiritual father. Thus Lev Gillet has advised that

> the Christian attracted by the Jesus Prayer and starting out on this particular spiritual way would therefore do well to disregard the psycho-physiological methods recommended by the monks of the past ... But every Christian can attain to the summits of the Jesus Prayer with no other 'technique' except that of love and obedience. It is the inner attitude that is here all important. The Jesus Prayer confers upon us freedom from everything except Jesus himself.[209]

Kallistos Ware examined the possibility of interaction between the hesychast tradition and non-Christian influences. He noted the striking parallels between hesychastic practices and Indian yoga. There are similarities to Meditation with a mantra or short formula, the use of physical postures (āsanas) and breathing practices (prāṇāyāma). But there are also differences as yoga is primarily a technique for concentration using natural powers.[210] He considered the possible influence of the Sufi Islamic practice of *dhikr*, the memory and invocation of the name of God. The similarities to the Jesus Prayer are close and appear much more likely than yoga to have had direct influence on hesychasm. *Dhikr* involves elaborate physical postures and breathing practices as well as movement of the prayer from the lips to the heart. Moreover, the invocation is addressed to the transcendent and personal God. The obvious difference is that the Jesus Prayer is a direct and specific invocation to Jesus the Divine Word Incarnate rather than simply an invocation to God.

Nonetheless, Ware thought that the similarities were so considerable that it seemed highly probable that there was some direct interaction. Although direct evidence is lacking there were many opportunities for such mutual influences.[211]

John Dupuche has also examined the question of Hindu or Islamic influence on hesychasm.[212] Discussing contacts between India and Sufism he noted that in the eighth and ninth centuries CE, wandering monks described as Indian were to be found in Mesopotamia and Syria. In the eleventh century, Hatha Yoga practitioners, Nath-yogins, were in Central Asia and Iran and had influence on the Sufi brotherhoods. By the twelfth century, *dhikr* involved practices including posture and breathing control.

Sufism may have acted as a bridge between India and the psychophysical practices of hesychasm.

Although there are inadequate documentary records in relation to the interaction between Sufism and Europe, there was opportunity for Muslims to easily interact with Jews and Christians during the seventh and eighth centuries CE. There was a great deal of contact between Europe and the Levant associated with the Crusades, and pilgrimages to the Holy Land or to Mecca resulted in a constant mixing of people. Further, there were also exchanges between Mount Sinai and the Christian East.[213]

The material discussed in this chapter would suggest that many of the features of the Jesus Prayer as it merges into *hesychia* may include some of the characteristics of Meditation. This applies only to the formal use of the prayer where it is practised for specified time periods, such as twenty or thirty minutes, and not the free form where it can be done in the course of performing other routine, day-to-day activities. It is apparent that simply at the level of technique, the Jesus Prayer shares some of the elements of mantra-style yoga Meditation. Nevertheless, it is at the same time vastly different, because it is addressed with faith to the Lord Jesus, the Christ and Incarnate Word of God, and it specifically evokes his presence in our hearts.

CHAPTER 6

Monasticism in the West

Depart from evil, and do good; seek peace, and pursue it.
Psalm 34:14

Western monasticism developed in the Benedictine tradition. Following the invasion of the Western Roman Empire by Germanic tribes, the Benedictine monasteries remained as havens of civilization and spirituality. In establishing his *Rule for Monasteries*, Benedict of Nursia (480–547) had been influenced by the previous contribution to monasticism of John Cassian. Jacques-Albert Cuttat, however, has perceived in the Rule of Saint Basil an emphasis on perpetual prayer which he did not detect in the Rule of Saint Benedict.[214] Cuttat considered that the practice of the invocation of the name of Jesus does not seem to have been formally handed down in the Latin Church.[215]

Living in communities, the Benedictines practised a coenobitic form of monasticism. In the Middle Ages, the Benedictine school of spirituality was centred on three major practices.[216] Remaining in their monasteries for life, the monks would labour in the fields where contact with God in nature was part of their religious experience, consistent with the principle that "to work is to pray" (*laborare est orare*). The second element was *lectio divina*, a practice based on reading the Scriptures slowly and reflectively. This form of prayerful reflection led the monk from his mind to his heart, deepening into meditation and contemplative prayer. The third major practice was the liturgical chanting of the Divine Office and celebrating the Eucharist.

Within Western monasticism there were also anchorites. In contrast to other monastic traditions, the Carthusian Order founded by Saint Bruno (c.1030–1101) consisted of small communities of hermits who had a minimal community life.[217] Embracing a life of radical separation from the world, the monks lived in solitude and silence. Their life was not escapism but a quest for total renunciation, seeking God alone. Each monk lived in his own hermitage in solitude although he was still part of a community. The description of one of the early priors, Guigo I (1083–1136), that a Carthusian must be "possessing quiet, devoted entirely to Christ" (*quietus Christo*) embodies the ideal of *hesychia*.[218]

The Carthusian community gathers in its church three times per day (at midnight for the night office, in the morning for Mass and in the late afternoon for Vespers). While their lives are spent almost totally in silence, there is some provision for communal gathering and recreation particularly on Sundays and Feast Days. *Lectio divina* is a central component of their life of prayer. To the bewilderment of many, in this rare vocation the monks do not engage in any active ministry in the wider church, such as preaching or administering the sacraments.

Lectio divina

The process of growth in prayer with *lectio divina* has four interrelated components.[219] The first stage is *lectio* (reading) in which a very short passage of Scripture is read slowly and lovingly. The second stage, called *meditatio*, involves focusing the thoughts, feelings and reflections on the chosen passage. The third stage of *oratio* is prayer arising out of the reflections on the scriptural passage. The fourth stage is *contemplatio*. As the name suggests, this latter stage involves mystical prayer in which human effort is superseded by experience of the divine presence and action. It involves what is referred to as "infused contemplation" in which God, in his sovereign freedom, gives his gifts of mystical graces as he sees fit. These mystical graces can only be passively received as no amount of active prayer or self-effort can produce such states of contemplation. This category of contemplation in the Latin Church of the West appears to correspond to the ineffable, self-acting and pure visionary states of prayer described by the Eastern Orthodox spiritual teachers. Spiritual writings sometimes refer to patterns of prayer which are non-verbal or free of conceptual thoughts. Although perhaps ineffable, such prayer practices may not necessarily include the more exalted states of infused contemplation.

It has been noted that John Cassian's synthesis of biblical *meditatio* and monologistic prayer with "ineffable ecstasy of the heart" describes a method of unceasing prayer which became central to later Byzantine mysticism. However, his contribution to the Latin tradition lies in his theology of prayer and teaching on spiritual knowledge in which the beginnings of the monastic practice of *lectio divina* can be discerned.[220]

By the twelfth century *lectio divina* was becoming viewed in terms of four sequential steps. The Carthusian Guigo II portrayed it as such in his book *Scala Claustralium*, the "ladder of monks" ascending to God. In the era of Scholasticism, the four steps tended to be seen as different types of prayer appropriate for different types of people. Contemplation came to be understood as a rare and exalted state suitable for spiritually advanced people such as monks and nuns in monasteries and not for ordinary laypeople.[221] Historical factors have reinforced this view, which has persisted into modern times.

At the time of the Reformation, the traditions of contemplation became even further isolated. While the Protestant reformers of the sixteenth century suppressed monasteries in many countries, the Catholic Inquisition pursued any mystical practices which raised suspicions about heretical tendencies. In the words of Thomas Ryan, "caught between these two hostile forces, contemplative life in the West went into hiding."[222] In the seventeenth century Quietism, a heretical mystical movement, arose and taught that spiritual perfection required passivity before God in contemplation, indifference, and annihilation of the will, and withdrawal from exterior good actions which were seen as useless for sanctification.

In the light of these broad historical trends, contemplative prayer was regarded as a rare vocation beyond the experience of the ordinary believer. This attitude persisted in the Catholic Church until the latter half of the twentieth century. A pioneer in the modern revival of contemplative prayer in the West was the Cistercian monk Thomas Merton (1915–68). An enormously prolific spiritual writer, Merton sought to present contemplation as something suitable for all Christians. Although not focusing on techniques or methods, he wrote extensively from his own experiences of prayer. He advocated an attitude conducive to contemplative prayer rather than a method or system. Two forms of contemplative prayer, Christian Meditation and Centering Prayer developed in the 1970s, will be considered in chapters 7 and 8 respectively.

The Cloud of Unknowing

In fourteenth-century Europe there was a strong resurgence of mysticism exemplified by the Rhineland mystics. During that century an anonymous author in England wrote a book on prayer and the spiritual life called *The Cloud of Unknowing*. Nothing is known specifically about the author, but he was clearly a monk devoted to contemplation. It has been suggested that he may have been a Carthusian. This work is an expression of the medieval spirituality of the West, and it is clearly much influenced by the apophatic mystical tradition expounded by Pseudo-Dionysius. This tradition, which emphasizes that God is best known through negation, was a prominent theme of the Eastern Church Fathers such as Gregory of Nyssa.

In the European West, during the medieval period in which *The Cloud* was written, Dionysius was thought to have been a convert of Paul writing to Timothy and hence seen as possessing very great authority. Modern scholarship has suggested that Pseudo-Dionysius was a Syrian monk, probably writing in the sixth century. The author of *The Cloud* was much influenced by his work *The Mystical Theology*, which taught that in addition to rational knowledge of God through philosophy and speculative theology relying upon affirmation, there is also a higher way of knowing God through negation, laying aside created things to approach God who transcends all creation.[223] Pseudo-Dionysius wrote:

> For this I pray; and, Timothy, my friend, my advice to you as you look for a sight of the mysterious things, is to leave behind you everything perceived and understood, everything perceptible and understandable, all that is not and all that is, and, with your understanding laid aside, to strive upward as much as you can toward union with him who is beyond all being and knowledge. By an undivided and absolute abandonment of yourself and

everything, shedding all and freed from all, you will be uplifted to the ray of the divine shadow which is above everything that is.[224]

William Johnston described *The Cloud* as being "part of a great current of mediaeval spirituality", noting that the author showed a striking similarity to the teachings of John of the Cross two centuries later. He concluded that both writers belong to a common apophatic tradition.[225]

In addition to being an important element in the tradition of contemplative prayer, *The Cloud* is very relevant to the theme of this book, because as will be discussed in chapters 7 and 8, it has been claimed in modern times to be a source of inspiration for the development of the practices of both Centering Prayer and Christian Meditation.

An examination of the teachings presented in *The Cloud* can enhance our understanding of these issues. It is noteworthy that the author of *The Cloud* emphasized that his book was not suitable for everyone. In the Foreword he insisted that whoever possesses the book was charged with a serious responsibility "not to read it, write or speak of it, nor allow another to do so, unless you really believe that he is a person deeply committed to follow Christ perfectly."[226] He wanted the book to be read only by persons who have resolved to follow Christ "into the inmost depths of contemplation".[227] The person who would benefit from his book is one who is engaged in the active Christian life and feeling "the mysterious action of the Spirit in their inmost being stirring them to love".[228] He stated that although these stirrings need not be a continual state, they should at least occur now and again "in the very core of their being".[229] He was clearly not writing for all and sundry but only for those well advanced in the ways of prayer who were capable of grasping his message.

The author also emphasized that parts of his book should not be considered selectively but seen in the broader context of the other chapters. Near the end of his book he repeated the admonitions he gave in the Foreword, emphasizing that the book should only be given to someone who could understand and appreciate it and that it was not suitable for others.[230] At the end of the book, in chapter 75, he described signs by which we can determine whether or not God is drawing us to contemplation.[231] Firstly, a person needs to have purified his/her conscience according to the precepts of the Church and the advice of a spiritual father.[232] The second sign was to be habitually attracted to simple contemplative prayer rather than other devotions. Another sign of God's call to the work of contemplation is the person finding no peace in inner or outer work, unless the principal concern was for one's love to be fixed upon *The Cloud of Unknowing*. Finally, a clear sign of being called to this work is an attitude of joy, deeper longing, and love in a person who detects the return of the gift of grace after it has receded for a time. God in his mercy does not look at what we have been but what we desire to be. Contemplative work is for those who have renounced the active life in the world;[233] patient struggle and endurance are required.[234]

The Cloud commences with an acknowledgement of the four stages of Christian life as steps in a sequence of spiritual growth.[235] The author urges the reader to relentlessly pursue a lively longing for God.[236] Until joy is experienced, perseverance is required in the face of darkness of the mind, "a cloud of unknowing", in which nothing is known or felt "except a naked intent towards God in the depths of your being".[237] The work of contemplation is not time-consuming as the will needs only a brief instant to turn to God. While God cannot be fully comprehended through knowledge, he can be embraced through love.[238] It is advised that while there is a "cloud of unknowing" above, between the person and God, a "cloud of forgetting" is to be fashioned below into which all created things are to be relegated.[239] Focusing on positive attributes is no longer of any use. Instead, the mind is to rest in awareness of God's "naked existence and to love and praise him for what he is in himself".[240] The author advised setting aside all that can be known under the "cloud of forgetting", and "yes, beat upon that thick *cloud of unknowing* with the dart of your loving desire and do not cease come what may".[241]

In chapter 7, he taught that even good thoughts are to be dispelled during prayer in favour of a naked desire for God alone. He suggested that:

> if you want to gather all your desire into one simple word that the mind can easily retain, choose a short word rather than a long one. The one syllable words such as 'God' or 'love' is best. But

choose one that is meaningful to you. Then fix it in your mind so that it will remain there come what may.[242]

Distracting thoughts are to be subdued by this one word alone, the value of which lies in its simplicity.[243] Ideas about God are not to distract the person from attentiveness to God himself.[244]

Two methods recommended for handling distractions are either to look beyond them as if looking over one's shoulder with longing for God, or to admit helplessness and surrender into God's hands.[245] The author speaks of three ascending stages from the active to contemplative life and advises that the human effort is to prepare for and respond to God's action "which is the awakening of love and which he alone can do".[246] It is emphasized that while contemplation is a free gift from God which our efforts cannot produce, it is not given to a person who has no aptitude for it.[247] It is stated clearly that "techniques and methods are ultimately useless for awakening contemplative love."[248]

The Cloud makes references to the components of *lectio divina* in chapter 35 in which it states that "anyone who aspires to contemplation ought to cultivate *Study, Reflection,* and *Prayer,* or to put it differently, reading, thinking, and praying."[249] It goes on to observe, however, that for those continually occupied in contemplation, their meditation is experienced differently and is "more like a sudden intuition or obscure certainty. Insight like this is more divine than human in origin."[250] Assuming a person is drawn by grace and has sought advice about leaving the earlier practices behind, it is sufficient to focus on a simple word "and without the intervention of analytical thought allow yourself to experience directly the reality it signifies".[251]

While advising contemplatives against wordy prayer, there is reference to the one little interior word "not merely spoken or thought but surging up from the depths of a man's spirit, the expression of his whole being".[252] The prayer of one syllable has the power "to pierce the heavens", because it is "the prayer of a man's whole being".[253] The author teaches that the mind and heart should be emptied of everything except God during the time of contemplation, because everything else is an obstacle between the person praying and God.[254] *The Cloud* teaches that while maintaining reverence for God's gifts, we should remain indifferent to all delights or consolations experienced in prayer which vary from person to person, "but God in his great wisdom determines what is best for each one".[255] It also notes that while our superficial self perceives contemplation as emptiness and darkness, "our true inner self appreciates it is a fullness beyond measure".[256] In chapter 70 the author alludes to his affinity to the apophatic theology of Pseudo-Dionysius with the words: "Anyone who reads Denis's book will find confirmed there all that I have been trying to teach in this book from start to finish."[257]

In the West, the *lectio divina* framework formed the basic foundation and context in which most contemplative prayer was practised. While the author of *The Cloud of Unknowing* acknowledged that the first three steps of *lectio*, *meditatio* and *oratio* are necessary preliminaries, his main focus was on the transition to *contemplatio* itself with the experience of "the blind work of contemplative love" produced within a person by God himself.[258] Although he described the contemplative process as work, it is not work in the normal sense of the word. It is not something we can produce by a deliberate act of will.[259] There is work involved, however, in becoming receptive to these touches of divine grace and in responding to them by relegating all created things under *the cloud of forgetting*. *Lectio divina* remained the main pattern of personal prayer within the religious orders. In chapter 9, we will discuss its expression in the Carmelite tradition as exemplified by Teresa of Avila and John of the Cross. In chapter 10, when we consider the Jesuit tradition, we will find that further modifications were developed by Ignatius Loyola.

CHAPTER 7

Christian Meditation

Be still, and know that I am God!
                                                            Psalm 46:10

In modern times some monks in the Benedictine tradition have developed innovative forms of apophatic prayer. The term "Christian Meditation" is widely used to refer to the method of Meditation advocated by a Benedictine monk, the late John Main (1926–82), and will be referred to as such in the following discussion. To understand Christian Meditation requires an examination of the life story of John Main.

Douglas Victor Main was born in London to Irish Roman Catholic parents. He took the religious name John years later, when he became a Benedictine monk. The fourth of six children, he grew up in a happy family.[260] At the age of eleven, he was accepted into London's Westminster Cathedral Choir School. In 1939, after the outbreak of World War II, he was evacuated to a Jesuit school north of London, where he stayed with family friends. In 1942, he began work as a student journalist at a suburban newspaper, but in the following year he enlisted in the Royal Corps of Signals, where he was assigned to a Wireless Communications Unit. After joining the Communications Intelligence Unit, he was assigned to a war theatre in Belgium in 1945, where his unit was often in danger behind retreating enemy lines.[261]

After returning to civilian life in 1946, he decided to study for the priesthood in the religious congregation of Canons Regular of the Lateran. He was assigned to study theology in Rome in 1949, but during the next year he left that congregation.[262] He subsequently studied law at Trinity College Dublin, an environment in which he flourished.[263]

In 1954, he applied to join the British Colonial Service. After taking up duties in Kuala Lumpur in 1955, he had a chance meeting with Swami Satyananda, a Hindu monk to whom he was delivering a goodwill message from the Governor. The Swami had founded an orphanage school and ashram. When asked by Main about the spiritual basis for his many good works, the Swami replied that it was his daily practice of Meditation. John Main was later to write:

> I was deeply impressed by his peacefulness and calm wisdom. For the Swami, the aim of Meditation was coming to awareness of the spirit who dwells in our hearts . . . who enfolds the whole universe, and in silence is loving to all.[264]

John Main asked the Swami to teach him to meditate. On his first visit to learn Meditation the Swami told him:

> To meditate, you must become silent. You must be still. And you must concentrate. In our tradition we know only one way in which you can arrive at that stillness, that concentration. We use a word that we call a mantra. To meditate, what you must do is to choose this word and then repeat it, faithfully, lovingly and continually. That is all there is to Meditation. I really have nothing else to tell you. And now we will meditate.[265]

The Swami pointed out that since John Main was a Christian, he needed to meditate with his Christian faith, and therefore he gave him a Christian mantra. John Main meditated with the Swami over a period of eighteen months. Returning to Dublin in 1956, he became Professor of International Law at Trinity College. In 1958, his eleven-year-old nephew's death from a brain tumour had an enormous effect on him, confronting him with questions of life, death and the purpose of existence. He wrote:

> As I reviewed my life at this time, I was forcibly struck by the fact that the most important thing in my entire existence was

my daily Meditation. I decided, therefore, to structure my life on Meditation and sought to do so by becoming a monk.[266]

He joined the Benedictine abbey at Ealing in London. Discussing his practice of Meditation with his Novice Master, he was directed to discontinue it in favour of prayer using words, thoughts, and images. Out of obedience he complied with this directive in a spirit of detachment. In 1962, after his novitiate, he was sent to study theology in Rome at the International Benedictine College of San Anselmo.

He was ordained to the priesthood at Ealing Abbey in 1963 and in the following year taught at St Benedict's Middle School at Ealing.[267] In 1969, he was assigned to Washington, DC, becoming headmaster at St Anselm's Benedictine Boys School. During his time in Washington he discovered the writings of John Cassian. He noted that in the *Conferences* on prayer, Cassian advocated the repetition of a short verse (*formula*) to lead into an interior silence. John Main believed that Cassian's *formula* represented the Christian *mantra* tradition of Meditation, which he had been practising for the previous twenty years. He concluded that the use of a mantra in contemplative prayer was part of ancient Christian tradition. John Main was delighted to discover that John Cassian was a major influence on Benedict, who urged his monks to read Cassian's writings.[268] After returning to Ealing Abbey in 1974, he received permission to establish a small lay community in the monastery grounds, which would incorporate the daily practice of Meditation. Among the young men joining this community was Laurence Freeman who, after the death of John Main in 1982, continued his work in promoting Christian Meditation.

In 1976, John Main began to explore the possibility of founding another contemplative community. In the following year, he received approval from Ealing to found a Benedictine community in Montréal, Canada, accompanied by Laurence Freeman. The new house that was opened in Montréal thrived, with increasing numbers of people coming there to engage in Meditation.

In September 1979, John Main developed abdominal pains, which were later diagnosed as being due to bowel cancer. Initially surgical treatment was successful. After recuperation he continued his teaching and writings, including conducting retreats and conferences in Ireland. However, in 1982, he experienced a relapse of symptoms which heralded advanced cancer. He initially responded well to radiotherapy and chemotherapy and managed to travel to Ireland and England. On returning to Canada where he now lived, his health declined, and he required palliative care. It was noted by his carers that in the final days before his death on 30 September 1982, he showed a spirit of detachment and a willingness to surrender to God through continual Meditation.[269]

Laurence Freeman had been ordained to the priesthood in 1979 and was a devoted student of John Main. He has subsequently continued the work of John Main as the Spiritual Guide and Director of the World Community for Christian Meditation. Over the years there has been a continuing proliferation of Meditation groups in many countries following John Main's tradition of Christian Meditation. Freeman has travelled extensively around the world, conducting teachings and Meditation retreats in many countries in the service of promoting the ideal of a "Monastery without Walls". Over the past three decades, Christian Meditation has been increasingly practised internationally within the Catholic Church and other Christian denominations.

The practice of Christian Meditation

John Main taught that his system of Christian Meditation was to be practised as follows:

> Sit down. Sit still and upright. Close your eyes lightly. Sit relaxed but alert. Silently, interiorly begin to say a single word. We recommend the prayer-phrase 'Maranatha'. Recite it as four syllables of equal length. Listen to it as you say it, gently but continuously. Do not think or imagine anything—spiritual or otherwise. If thoughts and images come, these are distractions at the time of meditation, so keep returning to simply saying the word. Meditate each morning and evening for between 20 and 30 minutes.[270]

In his book *Word into Silence*, first published in 1980, John Main elaborated on the theology and practice of Christian Meditation, which he had developed over the previous decade. In answer to the question of how we pray, he noted Paul's teaching that we do not even know how we ought to pray, but that the Spirit prays within us (Romans 8:26-7). For the Christian prayer is nothing less than entry into the prayer experience of Jesus himself.[271] He lamented that people who could not find this deeper spiritual teaching in the Church had been seeking it outside the Church in their thousands.

It was his view that rather than just mastering a technique, Meditation was more a learning to respond directly to the depths of our own nature.[272] He considered that we need to get in touch with ourselves first before we can turn openly to a relationship with God. Meditation helps us to be at peace with ourselves so we can then be at peace with God within us. He noted the message of Paul, indicating that the impact of the arrival of Jesus is a totally new creation because through him "we have obtained access to this grace in which we stand", and "God's love has been poured into our hearts through the Holy Spirit that has been given to us" (Romans 5:1-5). He saw Christian Meditation as allowing God's mysterious and silent presence within us to become the reality in our lives. It is a learning process to concentrate and to attend.[273] However, although most Christians recognized the inner presence of God at a theoretical level, often this truth did not really live in their hearts.

He taught that in Meditation we do not *think about* God or spiritual things, but we endeavour to *be with* God, to experience Him as the ground of our being. John Main emphasized the need to become more and more silent in order to commune with God dwelling within us. In the silence we need to listen, concentrate and attend rather than to think. We need to achieve a state of alert stillness in our mind and heart.[274]

He discussed the problem of distraction and "monkey chatter", mentioning the teachings of Cassian (*Conferences* 10.10) on the use of the constant repetition of his *formula* to eliminate distractions. He reported that reading Cassian reminded him of the repetitive prayer of the tax collector approved of by Jesus: "God, be merciful to me, a sinner!" (Luke 18:9-14).[275] It is interesting, however, that John Main focused on the repetition of the phrase rather than the content of the words. Nonetheless, he also noted the instruction of Jesus that in prayer we were not to "heap up empty phrases as the Gentiles do" (Matthew 6:7), prayer being not so much a matter of talking to God but of listening to and being with God.[276] He also noted the teaching of *The Cloud of Unknowing*: "We must pray in the height, depth, length and breadth of our spirit, not in many words but in a little word."[277]

John Main equated Cassian's *formula* with a *mantra*. He advised consultation with a teacher in choosing one's mantra but if not, one should choose a word within Christian tradition, such as "Jesus", "Maranatha" or "Abba". He taught that a word without mental associations for us helps our meditation to be free of all images. He admired Cassian's talk of becoming "grandly poor" (*egregius pauper*) by restricting the mind to the poverty of a single verse.[278] He saw Meditation as simplicity itself with renunciation of words, thoughts and imaginations.[279]

John Main saw prayer as involving the experience of being filled with the Spirit, and he viewed it as progressing in Meditation by a deepening fidelity to saying the mantra. He viewed such faithful repetition as integrating our whole being and bringing us to silence, concentration and the necessary level of consciousness to enable us to open our minds and hearts to the love of God working in the depths of our being. With progressive fidelity, the mantra begins to sound in our hearts and seems to be in the very depths of our being. The mantra was seen as simply a device leading to the Christian experience of the living Spirit of God within us.[280] He taught that it had the power to integrate mind and heart, deepening our wholeness and central harmony.

He saw Meditation as a process of self-discovery involving honesty, simplicity and shedding of our illusions. One aspect of advancing in self-knowledge is that it is accompanied by encounters with dark forces, fears and anxieties, which means there is a cycle of death and resurrection. What dies is everything that obstructs us from realizing life in its fullness while the discovery of our real self brings indescribable joy.[281]

Progress requires renouncing self to take up the cross but in doing so, we enter new depths of being incorporated into Christ (2 Corinthians 5:17). John Main stated that the mantra leads us in simplicity to experiencing the prayer of the Spirit in our heart. He did not think of Meditation as a technique as such, but a very simple means of leading to self-awareness and awareness of the Spirit praying "Abba, Father" in our hearts, the fruit of which is joy and peace.[282]

John Main noted that many Christians had lost touch with their own traditions of prayer. We need to realize that it is not a matter of us talking to God but rather God finding us.[283] He considered that the use of a mantra was part of Christian tradition, as exemplified by John Cassian and the author of *The Cloud of Unknowing*. He spoke of our fidelity to the mantra continuing to grow and become more deeply rooted in us. We begin saying the mantra in our minds, but it progresses to sounding in our hearts. We then begin to listen to it. He recalled his Hindu teacher likening this process to a man hearing a sound in a valley below while he toiled up the side of a mountain. The higher he reached up the mountainside, the fainter became the sounding from the valley below, requiring more attentive listening. Eventually the day comes when there is absolute silence and the mantra is no longer heard.[284]

John Main also described a potential pitfall in Meditation consisting of what Cassian referred to as *pax perniciosa*. This phenomenon is the experience of peace, or euphoria, which the person seeks to maintain, causing them to stop saying the mantra and thereby preventing progress. His repeated advice was simply: "Say your mantra."[285]

John Main also stressed how Meditation had implications for the strengthening of the Christian community. It involves transcending our egocentricity by reaching out in love for others. In his life this led to the development of a worldwide spiritual family.[286] In 1976 John Main gave his first public teaching on Christian Meditation in talks to the Trappist community at Gethsemane Abbey in Kentucky.[287] He spoke to fellow monks about his own spiritual journey. He related how when he was headmaster at St Anselm's School in Washington, D.C. a young man asked him to be taught something about Christian mysticism. As a result, he re-read Augustine Baker's *Holy Wisdom*.[288] This in turn led him to examine Cassian's *Conferences* and discover in them references to what he believed to be a mantra practice.[289]

In his second Gethsemane talk, John Main emphasized that Meditation is concerned with *being* rather than *thinking*. In his words: "Simply to be in His presence is all-sufficing." He also pointed out that in the poverty of Meditation, what we surrender and die to is not the self or the mind but rather the *image* of the self or the mind with which we mistakenly identify. We divest ourselves of the illusion of the ego "by concentrating on the real Self, created by God, redeemed by Jesus, the Temple of the Holy Spirit". The searchlight is turned off ourselves and onto *the Other*, but it is a prayer of faith, because we leave ourselves behind before *the Other* appears. This leap of faith is the risk involved in all loving.[290] In his third talk he warned against getting side-tracked by thinking about technique. With regard to the choice of a word to use as a mantra he recommended "Maranatha".[291]

The Foreword to his book *Moment of Christ* was the last thing written by John Main not many weeks prior to his death in 1982. As such, it comprises a beautiful and concise summation of his teachings.[292] In this brief piece, he recalled his conviction that the central message of the New Testament is that there is really only one prayer and that is the prayer of Christ; a stream of love flowing constantly between Jesus and his Father. Furthermore, the most important task for any human life is to become as open as possible to that stream. In it, we are swept out of ourselves into "this great cosmic river of love". In order to do this, we need to learn the way of silence and stillness which is a most demanding discipline. In our prayer we must pass beyond the ego, becoming so still and silent that we cease thinking about ourselves. In his words: "At prayer we must become like the eye that can see but that cannot see itself." He noted: "The mantra is simply a means of turning our attention beyond ourselves—a way of unhooking us from our own thoughts and concerns." One day the mantra will cease to sound, and we become lost in God's eternal silence. When this happens, we are not to possess the silence if we become aware that we are in that state. As the silence gradually becomes longer, we become absorbed in the mystery of God, but we must "return to the mantra as soon as we become self-conscious of the silence".

John Main's claim that a mantra form of Meditation was part of earlier Christian prayer tradition has been questioned. The first difficulty is that he has identified John Cassian's *formula* as a *mantra*. Cynthia Bourgeault has noted that Cassian's statement in relation to Psalm 69 (LXX) was not the explicit reference to a mantra practice which John Main considered it to be.[293] Cassian had gone on to explain that the *formula* carried with it a cry to God in the face of every danger. She suggested that Cassian was describing *cataphatic* rather than *apophatic* prayer. Rather than being used as a mantra, it was intended to work with the feelings, bringing the mind into the heart, which is the classic pathway from the cataphatic to the apophatic. She wrote:

> In classic Christian practice one does not immediately access the apophatic by simply tethering the faculties; one takes a more circuitous route of concentrating them and intensifying them until they are finally overwhelmed in the divine love.[294]

Hence she saw Christian Meditation as being slightly innovative in relation to the classical tradition, although she believed it was theologically compatible with it.

John Main also thought that a mantra practice was taught by the author of *The Cloud of Unknowing*. In his third Gethsemane talk he commented that "throughout *The Cloud of Unknowing* the author urges us to choose a word that is full of meaning; but once you have chosen it, to turn from the meaning and associations and to listen to it as sound. 'Maranatha' is a perfect mantra from that point of view."[295] While the author of *The Cloud* recommended a small meaningful word to use in prayer, he did not actually suggest that one should turn from its meaning and associations and listen to it simply as sound.

It appears that John Main may have been more innovative than he realized in developing Christian Meditation. He has utilized a mantra Meditation practice of Hindu origin and modified it for use as a Christian contemplative prayer. While repetitive prayer phrases such as the Jesus Prayer and the Hail Mary have certainly been a long-standing part of Christian prayer traditions, they were never meant to be recited merely as sounds or vibrations, or detached from the inherent meaning of their wording. Hence, they do not qualify as actual mantras. Despite these observations I recognize that Christian Meditation can be a helpful means of contemplative prayer for many people. Its widespread popularity among Catholics and other Christians indicates that it is meeting a significant need felt by many people in modern times for a deeper life of prayer and spirituality.

CHAPTER 8

Centering Prayer

He will cover you with his pinions,
and under his wings you will find refuge.
Psalm 91:4

Centering Prayer is another apophatic style of prayer developed by a small group of Trappist (Cistercian) monks at St Joseph's Abbey, Spencer, Massachusetts, in the early 1970s. This occurred at a time when many young people were turning to Eastern religions and their Meditation practices.

A simple openness to God

The method of the prayer consists in utilizing a sacred word to open one's consciousness towards God and returning to that word and using it to let go of thoughts or other perceptions when they arise, thereby refocusing on a "bare, formless openness to God".[296] In the words of Fr Basil Pennington OCSO:

> Be with God within.
> Use a word to stay.
> Use the word to return.[297]

Aware that the Christian contemplative tradition in the West had to a large extent declined, particularly after the Reformation, these monks sought to help revive the contemplative dimension of the gospel.[298] In 1975, one of the monks, William Meninger, established the definitive method of Centering Prayer largely based on his reading of *The Cloud of Unknowing*. It was a way of presenting the Christian contemplative path in a Meditation method accessible to modern people.[299] Basil Pennington joined in this work, first publishing his book *Centering Prayer* in 1980,[300] though one of the most prolific writers on the subject was Thomas Keating (see below). After a more intensive experience of Centering Prayer, a number of support groups grew up, and in 1984 Contemplative Outreach Ltd. was established as a resource to provide support and training opportunities in relation to this method.

Thomas Keating

Thomas Keating wrote numerous books on the theme of Centering Prayer. Of particular relevance is a trilogy that begins with *Open Mind, Open Heart*. This book discusses Centering Prayer as a preparation for the gift of contemplation. Emphasizing that in Christianity, contemplative prayer was never meant to be a purely privatized experience, a second book, *The Mystery of Christ*, attempts to integrate the practice of contemplative prayer within the celebration of the liturgical year and living the Christian life. A third book, *Invitation to Love*, offers the conceptual background to the prayer practice.

In *Open Mind, Open Heart* the central elements of Centering Prayer are described. The meditator is advised to take up a comfortable position which will enable him or her to sit still for the duration of the meditation. With eyes closed, the meditator starts slowing the flow of thoughts by gently focusing on a chosen "sacred word", but the word is not meant to be repeated continuously. As often as further thoughts occur, the meditator returns to the sacred word as the expression of intent to consent to God's presence within.[301]

Centering Prayer involves detachment from "thoughts", which Keating defined as "an umbrella term for every perception, including body sensations, sense perceptions, feelings, images, memories, plans, reflections, concepts, commentaries, and spiritual experiences".[302]

The prayer involves the opening of one's whole being to God, who is beyond the psychological content of the present moment.[303] It involves effortlessness and letting go; a practice of intent rather than focused attention. The meditator gently returns to the sacred word whenever he or she becomes aware of becoming engaged in thoughts. The sacred word is a way of letting go of all thoughts and it makes it possible for the spiritual faculties to move towards interior silence.[304] Keating indicated that the principal focus in Centering Prayer is to deepen our relationship with Jesus Christ and through Him, with the Holy Trinity. The sacred word is designed to foster a receptive attitude.[305] Keating described the prayer as "listening to God, listening to silence, which is God's first language".[306] He taught that in this prayer God speaks in the silence to our inmost being without our knowing it.[307]

Another characteristic feature of Centering Prayer is its reputed capacity to purify the unconscious mind. Emotional residues in the unconscious emerge during the prayer and Keating taught that with practice a person's psychic wounds are healed.[308] The Spirit is "removing the emotional junk of a lifetime that is inside of us".[309]

In the Preface to *The Mystery of Christ*, Keating explained that contemplative prayer and liturgy enrich each other and together they further the gospel's call to conversion.[310] He explained that the word "mysteries" of Christ refers to the redeeming actions of Jesus, particularly his passion, death, and resurrection, and the sacraments which prolong his activities in time through the ministry of the Church. The visible actions of the sacraments are signs which contain his presence and action here and now. To highlight the meaning of ritual, he cited the vivid example of the Gospel story of the woman afflicted with a haemorrhage (Mark 5:30). He suggested that the sacramental rituals are "the clothing of God, so to speak, and are saturated with the healing power of God". He made an analogy between the humble faith of the woman who touched the cloak of Jesus and our celebration of the liturgy. Just as the healing power of Jesus went out from him to the woman, his healing power goes out when we approach the sacred rituals with faith.

In his book, Keating discussed the liturgical year, which focuses on the three great theological themes of divine light, life and love. Each celebration of the Eucharist contains all these themes, but in the liturgical year they are expanded to enable them to be focused on and celebrated one by one. The book examines in turn the Christmas–Epiphany Mystery, the Easter-Ascension Mystery, and Pentecost and Ordinary Time. Keating emphasized that the liturgy enables us to perceive the mysteries of Christ not only as historical events but as his manifestation in the present. He suggested that the best preparation for this living contact is the regular practice of contemplative prayer. Christ becomes present within us in the Eucharist, and from there we are commanded to preach the gospel to all creation and transform the world.

Prayer as therapy

In writing *Invitation to Love* Keating emphasized the need to take into account knowledge gained from psychology, especially the question of healing and transformation of the unconscious complexes and motivations underlying what he described as the "false self".

Drawing on insights from modern psychoanalytic thinking, he described how in our early lives we develop characteristic and habitual emotional patterns in reaction to and in compensation for traumas and day-to-day frustrations. This creates distortions to our "emotional programs" for happiness. Three main patterns of personality functioning tend to emerge, centring on the needs for survival/security, affection/esteem and power/control. These unconscious programs give rise to a false self which is always wounded.

In the face of circumstances that frustrate these unconscious motivations, the false self expresses itself as afflictive emotions such as anger, grief, fear, pride, greed, envy, lust and apathy. In its more extreme forms, the false self would manifest in what modern psychiatry recognizes as personality disorders.[311] Nevertheless we have all acquired a false self to some degree. This can be seen theologically as part of the human condition in accord with the doctrine of the fall. The spiritual path includes both the progressive dismantling of the false self and a struggle against sin which is a symptom of it. Keating observed that sessions of Intensive Centering Prayer often generated an outpouring of strong emotions and the surfacing of painful and repressed memories. Witnessing this "unloading of the unconscious", he discovered that regular practice of Centering Prayer had a healing effect which he termed "divine therapy".

He found that in his words, "This prayer heals the emotional wounds of a lifetime."[312] On the other hand, he did not deny that sometimes a person requires professional psychotherapy; Centering Prayer was nonetheless therapeutic at the psychological level in promoting the dismantling of the false self as well as deepening a person's relationship with God.

He wrote that a spiritual struggle is needed to address our unconscious motivations and unless that occurs the false self will stay with us in any situation.[313] For example, it will surface again after the initial fervour of a religious conversion.[314] The conscious resolution to change our behaviour is not enough to alter the unconscious value system and behaviour of the false self, but he considered that the passive purification of contemplative prayer can effect a profound spiritual healing.[315]

Cynthia Bourgeault has written about the need to develop spiritual awareness of an authentic self, deeper than that of our usual, ego-based perspective. She has likened this to "a kind of interior compass whose magnetic north is always fixed on God".[316] The true spiritual self perceives through a deeper, intuitive awareness. She also considered that Centering Prayer belongs to a surrender method of Meditation rather than concentrative or awareness methods. This method is very simple and consists of letting go of any thoughts that emerge into consciousness. The gesture of release is the essential feature, accompanied by what *The Cloud of Unknowing* describes as a "naked intent direct to God". What occurs during the prayer happens "in secret" and is deeper than the conscious mind. The sacred word is not a mantra, because it is not repeated constantly, and its role is merely to help with the release of thoughts.

Bourgeault has also highlighted the fact that Centering Prayer is not cataphatic prayer, which involves focused and concentrated work using our cognitive processes. On the contrary, it is apophatic, relying on spiritual awareness and bypassing the mental processes of reasoning, imagination, memory, emotion and visualization, and the sense of self attached to them.[317] She also pointed out that for the ego, Meditation is like a "mini-death", not at the level of the will but in terms of our core sense of identity. Theologically there is an element of self-emptying (*kenosis*) during the prayer.[318] Another important observation is that despite its therapeutic action, Centering Prayer is not meant to be simply psychological therapy. Further spiritual progress requires the transcending of egoism and the dismantling of the false self.[319] The spiritual journey involves acquiring self-knowledge gained through increased awareness of our mixed motivations and the dark aspects of our personalities.

Centering Prayer and *The Cloud of Unknowing*

The Cistercian monks who developed the practice of Centering Prayer have indicated that it expresses the teachings of *The Cloud of Unknowing*. There is no doubt that these Cistercians have drawn extensively from *The Cloud* in their promotion of Centering Prayer as a form of contemplative prayer suitable for modern times. William Meninger has written spiritual reflections clearly inspired by *The Cloud*, a book which he stated he had read over one hundred times.[320] Basil Pennington considered Centering Prayer to be a renewal of an ancient Christian prayer form.[321] By drawing together numerous references within the text he reconstructed a method which he considered constituted the precise form of prayer that the author taught to his disciple. The following elements were seen as corresponding to various chapters from *The Cloud*:

- Simply sit relaxed and quiet (chapter 44).
- It is simply a spontaneous desire springing towards God (chapter 4).
- Direct all your attention and yearning towards God as your sole concern (chapter 3).
- Only a brief moment is needed to turn desire towards its object (chapter 4).
- To focus all your desire choose a short word, preferably a single syllable like "God" or "love" but one that is meaningful to you (chapter 7).
- Never strain the mind or imagination (chapter 4).
- Preferably the word is to be wholly interior without associated sound or concepts (chapter 40).
- The little word represents God in all his complete fullness (chapter 40).

- When distracted from God, quickly return to recollection (chapter 4).
- If troubled by persistent annoying thoughts, answer with the one word (chapter 7).
- During prayer abandon thoughts of all created things (chapter 5).

Such an extensive list of attributes would seem to suggest that Centering Prayer closely reflects the teachings of *The Cloud*. Nonetheless the text itself indicates the author's very great concern that his work should only come into the hands of persons deeply committed to following Christ perfectly, who have already begun to experience the beginnings of a divine call to contemplation.[322] It would appear that the author would not favour sharing his teachings about the practice of contemplative prayer indiscriminately to people who have not gone through the necessary preliminary steps of a devout life and discursive forms of meditation according to the *lectio divina* sequence. His intended readership are people having already advanced far in the ways of prayer, who feel themselves being strongly drawn into the depths of contemplation by God's grace. It is unclear whether the author's concern that his teachings only be divulged to those suitably prepared is consistent with the opinion of Keating that "contemplation is a fundamental constituent of human nature and hence available to every human being".[323] This would also depend upon whether contemplation is defined as a state of infused mystical prayer.

Basil Pennington has depicted Centering Prayer as evolving from within the same desert tradition of prayer as that of John Cassian, *The Cloud of Unknowing* and the Jesus Prayer.[324] Despite acknowledging that precise instructions on the way of prayer were not explicitly spelt out in *The Cloud*, he considered there were repeated allusions in the text to such instructions. He concluded that by drawing together these elements it was possible to obtain a rather complete reconstruction of the prayer method.[325] Notwithstanding the various items identified by Pennington, it would seem uncertain whether the method which he described fully corresponds to that intended by the author. One could question, for example, how well the use of a sacred word as a symbol of intention which one only returns to when distracted by thoughts, compares with the statement in chapter 39 of *The Cloud*, which recommends ardent and fiery prayer concentrated in one word. None of these considerations is to argue that Centering Prayer is not a beneficial practice, but the extent to which it can be said to fully represent the teachings of *The Cloud* is less certain. In chapter 12 of this book, I will discuss criticisms that have been raised about the practice of Centering Prayer.

CHAPTER 9

The Carmelite Tradition

Your head crowns you like Carmel,
and your flowing locks are like purple;
a king is held captive in the tresses.
                    Song of Solomon 7:5

In the second millennium new religious orders arose in the West. Pre-eminent among them were the Carmelites, devoted to a life of prayer. The Carmelite tradition has made an enormous contribution to the prayer practices and spirituality of the Latin Church. While it is impossible to do justice to the tradition in a small book such as this, it is possible to give a brief overview of some of the key contributions. Of particular relevance are the teachings of Teresa of Avila on prayer and those of John of the Cross on the spiritual life.

From Mount Carmel to Europe

The Carmelite Order commenced in about 1200 on Mount Carmel, near the modern city of Haifa. Some lay hermits settled in a ravine near the fountain of Elijah. The Carmelite *Formula of Life*, a simple way of life in the spirit of the prophet Elijah, was approved by Albert, the Latin Patriarch of Jerusalem.[326] The *Formula*, in a revised form, became their rule in 1247. They were a small community of hermits, each one having his own cell separated from the others. They lived a life of solitude, silence and simplicity, and they performed manual labour. They held a weekly meeting and also gathered for a daily Eucharist. Although no detailed methods of prayer appear in the *Formula* and there are no accounts of the prayer of the hermits, it is reasonable to speculate that some of these hermits may have practised prayer similar to that of the Desert Fathers.[327] Nonetheless a pattern in the spirit of *lectio divina* is suggested in chapter 7 of the Rule of St Albert:

> Let all remain in their cells, or near them, meditating day and night on the Law of the Lord and keeping vigil in prayer, unless occupied with other lawful duties.[328]

Due to the emergence of hostile conditions for the Latin Kingdom of Jerusalem with the rise of Islam, many of the Carmelite hermits moved to continental Europe at a time when the eremitic life there was diminishing and being replaced by the mendicant way of life of the Dominican and Franciscan orders. These new orders were not confined to the stability of monasteries, but they were mobile and international in their ministries in the urban centres of Europe. The Carmelite lifestyle became modified with less silence and isolation and a more communal life. The loss of the solitude and stillness of Mount Carmel made it inevitable that the prayer practice of the Carmelite Friars would change.[329] Nonetheless, during this period Carmelites became more conscious of the implications of their heritage of having been founded on Elijah's mountain. Their charism, continuing the tradition of Elijah and Elisha as lovers of solitude and contemplation, also suggested a prophetic dimension.

In the fourteenth century, Felip Ribot, a Carmelite Provincial in Catalonia, left writings emphasizing that Carmelite prayer was based on solitude and a mystical orientation to prayer. He emphasized offering to God a pure heart and experiencing something of the power and bliss of the divine.[330] Although mystical phenomena are a special gift from God and cannot be earned through human effort, the Carmelites focused on becoming prepared and open to the graces of contemplation. In the sixteenth century, the great Spanish Carmelite mystic Teresa of Avila (1515–82) in collaboration with John of the Cross (1542–91) undertook a major reform of the Carmelite Order, producing the Discalced branch of the Carmelites. Teresa renewed the tradition of solitude for prayer and contemplation.

A later reform of the Carmelite Order of the Ancient Observance known as the Touraine reform resulted in desert houses occurring in both branches of the order. Followers of the Touraine reform favoured the practice of prayer of aspiration. The pre-eminent leader of this reform was a blind lay-brother, John of St Samson (1571–1636). He taught the practice of prayer in the form of fervent aspirations of love containing few words directed to God. Such aspirational prayer necessarily included the recurring mindfulness of God's presence. It emphasized the paramount importance of love in contemplative prayer. The Discalced Carmelite Brother Lawrence of the Resurrection (1614–91) was also a highly influential spiritual guide, producing a small and popular text *The Practice of the Presence of God*.[331]

A very important more recent Carmelite spiritual teacher was Thérèse of Lisieux (1873–94), who in her short life advocated a "Little Way" of living daily life with love and trust in God. She taught that sanctity can be achieved in the ordinary tasks of day-to-day life. She stated that: "Jesus does not demand great actions from us but simply surrender and gratitude."[332] She wrote that although she was sustained in her prayer by the Holy Scriptures, especially the Gospels, she reached a stage in which books became useless to her:

> I understand and I know from experience that: *'The kingdom of God is within you.'* Jesus has no need of books or teachers to instruct souls; He teaches without the noise of words. Never have I heard him speak, but I feel that he is within me at each moment; He is guiding and inspiring me with what I must say and do.[333]

Saints Teresa, John and Thérèse have all now been officially declared Doctors of the Church.

Saint Teresa of Avila

Teresa of Avila took the name "Teresa of Jesus" when she commenced her reform of the Carmelite Order. One of the pre-eminent spiritual teachers within Christianity, her writings on prayer and contemplation are of great importance. The teachings on prayer are mainly contained in two of her works, *The Way of Perfection* and *The Interior Castle*.

In *The Interior Castle*, which is the later work, the spiritual journey is described in terms of the image of a castle made of crystal or diamond containing seven concentric layers of dwellings or mansions, with an inner chamber representing the secret meeting place between God and the soul.[334] Moving progressively from the exterior into the central chamber of the castle represents the broad contours of the journey to union with God. When travelling through the first three dwellings, human effort is the predominant factor in rendering a person receptive to receive God's gift of contemplation. From the fourth dwellings onwards, the initiative comes entirely from God who bestows his gifts in total freedom.

In the first dwellings, as described by Teresa, we are distracted by superficial things which lack ultimate value, such as honour and prestige, unnecessary possessions, and disordered attachments. Forward movement is generated by humility, detachment and love for others. People in the first dwellings are susceptible to temptations from outside, which Teresa likens to poisonous creatures. In the second dwellings, hard work and spiritual struggle is required to progress with God's help. In reaching the third dwellings, a person has made progress, but there are the dangers of complacency and attachment to spiritual consolations. In the fourth dwellings, there is a shift from active prayer to God's free gift of so-called "infused" prayer.

Contemplation starts with *Recollection*, in which God gathers and quietens the mental faculties as a person's prayer progresses beyond active use of imagination, meditations and verbal expressions.[335] At this stage Teresa emphasizes that we are "not to think much but to love much" (IC 4.1.7).[336] Using the metaphor of human romantic love, descriptions of the fifth dwellings refer to brief and intermittent occurrences of the *Prayer of Union* with God, which is likened to God and the soul being engaged in a courtship. To illustrate the deeper transformation that is developing, Teresa introduces the image of a silkworm being transformed into a butterfly. The ugly silkworm spins a cocoon in which it encloses itself and seemingly dies only to emerge as a beautiful butterfly. Love of neighbour is the fruit of the development of true union with God.

In the sixth dwellings there are many mystical phenomena becoming manifested. The soul is depicted there as entering into a spiritual betrothal. This deeper union also engenders great suffering as the person experiences further purification. In the seventh dwellings the person attains spiritual marriage with permanent peace and union with God, the Holy Trinity. Having achieved this state a person still continues reaching out and serving others in the divine love (IC 7.4.6).[337]

The Way of Perfection is a book of instructions in which Teresa teaches the way of prayer for her nuns. It is very noteworthy that the explicit teaching on prayer does not begin until the second half of this book.[338] In this way Teresa indicates powerfully that three essential virtues are the indispensable prerequisites before a person can hope to receive the divine gift of contemplative prayer. Before elaborating on methods of prayer, Teresa insists on the vital necessity for the virtues of humility, love for one's neighbour, and detachment from all created things. In addition to these three necessary virtues Teresa added a fourth requirement, described emphatically as a "very determined determination" (*muy determinada determinación*) (WP 21.2).[339] These four qualities form the foundation to the transition from active prayer into contemplation. It is important to realize that in these teachings Teresa is not being a finger-wagging moralist. On the contrary, she is pragmatically pointing out essential prerequisites to progressing into deeper contemplative prayer.

It is clear that Teresa was not only teaching about methods of prayer but also about the profound personal transformation required to grow in prayer. Teresa saw love as essential to real community living. It was commanded by Jesus himself. It is the only reliable indicator or proof of genuine prayer, because prayer cannot be measured merely by subjective feelings. Selfless love for one's neighbour underpins the inner freedom enabling us to give ourselves to God. Hence love is "both the fruit and proof of authentic prayer and its foundation".[340]

Detachment is a process of acquiring freedom from being possessed by things other than God. It is therefore an essential element in acquiring love for Him. Detachment must apply to what is within us as well as to external things. Ultimately this requires readiness to renounce our own will for the sake of serving God.

Discussing humility, Teresa taught that "this whole building has humility as its foundation. If humility is not genuinely present, for your own sake the Lord will not construct a high building lest that building fall to the ground." (IC 7.4.8).[341] The favours in prayer which truly come from God "bring humility with them and always leave us with more light by which we may see our own unworthiness" (WP 39.5).[342] Instead of human honour (*honra*), whether from wealth, titles, rank, age or seniority, we should seek the honour of God. In her words: "the soul's profit and what the world calls honour can never go together" (WP 36.3).[343] She marvelled at the humility of God expressed in the Incarnation of Christ (WP 33.2.5)[344] and described coming to a sudden realization that "God is supreme Truth and to be humble is to walk in truth, for it is a very deep truth that of ourselves, we have nothing good but only misery and nothingness" (IC 6.10.7).[345]

Teresa's emphasis on determination highlights the need for a radical commitment to God for anyone seeking to advance in prayer. Addressing her nuns, she advocated perseverance and patience despite hardship: "Be determined, Sisters, that you came to die for Christ, not to live comfortably for Christ" (WP 10.5).[346] It is interesting that she taught that spiritual consolations and mystical graces are given by God to assist our perseverance and are not merely for our enjoyment. In her words: "I hold for certain that these favours are meant to fortify our weakness ... that we may be able to imitate him in his great sufferings" (IC 7.4.4).[347]

Teresa's image of the silkworm disappearing into the cocoon and emerging as a butterfly is her metaphor for the transformation involved in the path to union with God. Her teachings suggest that following the commandments and practising the essential virtues are the foundation to entering deeper states of prayer and contemplation. At the same time, they are also the fruit of deeper prayer through the gift of God's grace. Although God's absolute freedom is expressed in any way he wishes, such as his revelation to Saul on the road to Damascus, in the normal course of events practising the four qualities identified by Teresa are indispensable to making progress in the path of prayer and spiritual transformation.

Teresa refers to the first stage of prayer as "vocal prayer" in the sense that it involves words, whether spoken aloud or produced silently. They include liturgical prayers and prayers composed by others. She was insistent on the importance of saying vocal prayer well. She stated that she had known many people who, in practising vocal prayer, had been raised by God to the higher kind of contemplation.[348]

Discussing deeper mental forms of prayer, Teresa emphasized the need to increasingly focus our attention upon God. She stated: "for mental prayer in my opinion is nothing else than an intimate sharing between friends; it means taking time frequently to be alone with him whom we know loves us" (BL 8.5).[349]

Teresa noted that some people cannot practise recollection or concentrate their minds in meditation. She emphasized that when reciting a standard prayer such as the Lord's Prayer, it should not be a mere recitation of words repeated out of habit. There is a need for our minds to be thinking of the Lord who taught this prayer. We need to be aware of who it is that we are addressing. In referring to the problem of being distracted by irrelevant thoughts in saying the Lord's Prayer, she suggested that "the best remedy I have found for it is to try to fix my mind on the person by whom the words were first spoken" (WP 24.6).[350]

Teresa's definition of mental prayer includes what writers of her time referred to as meditation, involving active, discursive reflections using imagination and intellect. This meditation would lead into more affective prayer and personal communication with Christ. Whereas this type of prayer predominantly involved a person's own efforts aided by grace, Teresa saw contemplation as something that can only come as a free gift from God. Contemplation involved wordless awareness of the presence of Christ without the use of the intellect or imagination.[351]

The transition from meditation to contemplation commences in what Teresa referred to as *Recollection*. This consists of the gathering of mental faculties of intellect, will, memory and imagination focused within to meet Christ in prayer (WP 28.4).[352] Teresa showed some inconsistency in her terminology. Her descriptions suggest that she recognized a distinction between two types of recollection. One type of recollection could be called *acquired* while another type of recollection is *infused or God-given*. In chapters 26 to 29 of *The Way of Perfection* Teresa discussed *acquired recollection*.[353] Teresa noticed that a change took place as recollection became aided by a sense of being drawn passively into the depths; thus this prayer possesses both active and passive qualities.[354] She advised that we look at Christ who is always present, and that we "represent the Lord himself as close to you and behold how lovingly and humbly he is teaching you" (WP 26.1).[355]

In these comments she points to the need to become aware of his presence with attentiveness. It is not discursive meditation with imagination or reflections about Christ:

> I am not asking you now that you think about him or that you draw out a lot of concepts or make long and subtle reflections with your intellect. I am not asking you to do anything more than look at him. (WP 26.3)[356]

As an aid to this process she suggested beholding the representation of Christ in different moments of his life, such as seeing him on the way to the garden when we are sad or seeing him as risen when we are joyful. She was not suggesting imaginative explorations of such scenes, but simply describing a way to remain attentive and focused. This process is still predominantly human work, but it sets a necessary stage for the gift of contemplation, which is introduced by God in the fourth dwellings as infused recollection. It is then God's action.[357] Teresa suggested that during this active form of recollection we pray with our gaze fixed on Christ. This was seen as an easy way leading into the deeper stage of infused contemplation, *The Prayer of Quiet* (WP 28.4).[358]

Teresa insisted that simply practising a method of acquired recollection is not enough. For transformation to occur, the three essential virtues cannot be bypassed. Although God is totally free to act however he wishes, we cannot presume or expect divine intervention without our practice of the virtues (WP 16.6).[359] Advancement in prayer requires increasing detachment from things that enslave us and prevent a deepening relationship with God.

Saint John of the Cross

John of the Cross wrote of prayer in terms of only two broad categories, which he called *meditation* and *contemplation*. He did not refer to acquired or active *recollection*. He understood meditation as involving the use of our faculties in a self-directed activity, whereas contemplation involved infused light and love that are the pure gifts of God.[360] José de Quiroga (1562–1628), an early Discalced Carmelite writer, in describing a method of mental prayer which he attributed to John, outlined a process which suggests the possibility of acquired contemplation. This process involves three steps: firstly the representation of some mysteries; secondly, pondering them; and thirdly, experiencing the result in "an attentive and loving quietude before God".[361] This method was believed to lead to passing moments of contemplation which became increasingly more prominent and coalesced into a habit or state of contemplation.[362] This interpretation is disputed by Arraj, who has argued that John of the Cross recognized a sharp distinction between all forms of ordinary prayer or meditation and infused contemplation which, although having various degrees, is a gift from God which cannot be received through our own efforts.[363]

In his writings John of the Cross did not concentrate on methods of prayer, but he wrote extensively about the spiritual path itself. He used the imagery of darkness to describe the sense of obscurity, loss and deprivation occurring on the path of prayer. According to his teachings the experiences of "the dark night of the soul" are caused by God's increasing self-communication to a person progressing in the spiritual life. It involves purifications which arise firstly at the level of the senses, and later at the level of the spirit.[364]

It is unfortunate that John has been widely misunderstood and misrepresented, sometimes being depicted as fanatical in his asceticism and morbid in his approach to suffering. The metaphor of "the dark night" can conjure up thoughts of depression and misery. Such a view, however, is a gross distortion both of John's message of ecstatic love expressed in his poetry and writings, and the evidence that he was a gentle, loving man, widely sought after as a spiritual father.[365] He is considered by many to have composed the finest poems in the Spanish language. Most of his prolific writing was undertaken to provide commentaries on his poems, which describe the spiritual path through symbols and metaphors. In reference to John's famous poem "The Dark Night" (*Noche Oscura*), Peter Tyler has commented:

> The first thing to notice about the poem is that John calls it a "song of the soul's happiness" as the soul passes into "union with the beloved". This is no depression or suicidal imagery. This is the ecstatic voice of one who has reached the furthest limits of human existence.[366]

This path inevitably involves trials and suffering as well as joy.

It is noteworthy that in "The Dark Night" the soul's journey is described as driven by love:

> One dark night,
> fired with love's urgent longings.[367]

Furthermore, the darkness is not depicted as a negative development, even though it is associated with the suffering of purification. It is significant that in referring to this night John uses the word *oscura* to indicate the darkness. Gerald G. May, a psychiatrist, has observed that John's use of this word for darkness does not have sinister connotations but simply means obscure, unknown or mysterious.[368] The *dark night* is also described in the same poem as "a glad night", "a guiding night", "a night more lovely than the dawn", and "a night that has united the lover with his beloved".[369] This darkness is clearly healing and transformative. By contrast, another word, *tinieblas*, would have been used to describe a gloomy and sinister darkness.

Even when painful, the *dark night* referred to by John is given by God for our protection. As he explained: "Simple faith is necessary in seeking God. In outward things, light helps to prevent one falling; but in the things of God just the opposite is true: it is better for the soul not to see if it is to be more secure."[370] Using a psychological framework, Thomas Keating saw these trials as focusing on the core of the false self, as they involve the issues of seeking of pleasure, the need for control, and the need for security and certainty. He suggested that by letting go of our desires for satisfaction in these areas we consent to God's action in dismantling the false self.[371]

John differentiated *active* and *passive* nights. The former involve human efforts such as self-restraint, asceticism and practising the virtues, while in the latter it is God's action. A similar active and passive dichotomy is evident in the writings of both John and Teresa in contrasting meditation with contemplation. While this differentiation is important, it may be somewhat simplistic to contrast these aspects too sharply. Even our active efforts are not unconnected to the workings of God's grace, while his gratuitous action in contemplation encompasses human input in the sense of a receptive response to the divine actions. The notion of *synergy* would appear to be a useful way of thinking of this mutual interaction.

John indicated that the first sign of the *dark night* is the development of diminished interest in both spiritual things and things of the world. Persons in this state no longer enjoy their previous spiritual consolations. The *dark night* is the first step to contemplation, and it is divided into two parts: the *night of the senses* and the *night of the spirit*. According to John, the first sign to indicate the *night of the senses* is the development of aridity and dissatisfaction in prayer and spiritual things:

> As these souls do not get satisfaction or consolation from the things of God, they do not get any out of creatures either. Since God puts a soul in this dark night in order to dry up and purge its sensory appetite, he does not allow it to find sweetness or delight in anything.[372]

The second sign is that notwithstanding this dryness and aridity, the person remains deeply committed to serving God. This shows John's psychological insight in realizing that there are causes such as physical ailments or depression which can cause generalized dissatisfaction and loss of motivation. The presence of the second sign helps to exclude such non-spiritual factors.

The third sign is the inability of the person to engage in discursive forms of meditation which they had hitherto practised. In John's words,

> The powerlessness, in spite of one's efforts, to meditate and make use of the imagination, the interior sense, as was one's previous custom. At this time God does not communicate himself through the senses as he did before, by means of the discursive analysis and synthesis of ideas but begins to communicate himself through pure spirit by an act of simple contemplation, in which there is no discursive succession of thought.[373]

John also describes burdensome temptations and trials occurring during this dark night, consisting of sexual temptations ("the spirit of fornication"), thoughts of blasphemy, and a state of perplexity, scrupulosity and a dizzy spirit (*spiritus vertiginis*) (DN 1.14.1–3).[374] He indicated that these trials are sent by God to prepare the soul for wisdom and he noted that "by these trials it is truly humbled in preparation for its coming exaltation" (DN 1.14.4).[375] As observed by Gerald May, psychologically these disturbances represent either a desperate attempt to seek gratification, rage against God for the deprivations experienced, or disorientation at the changes that have occurred.[376] *The Carmelite Directory of the Spiritual Life* advises the adoption of an attitude of surrender. It states that persons placed in the *night of sense* should patiently bear the trials, refrain from their previous meditation practice but remain faithful to recollection and prayer until the Lord elevates them to higher states. It also advises them to consult a learned spiritual director for proper guidance during these trials.[377]

The *dark night of spirit* is yet a further stage of transformation, a deeper night preparing the soul for mystical union. In the memorable words of John of the Cross:

> This dark night is an inflow of God into the soul, which purges it of its habitual ignorances and imperfections, natural and spiritual, and which the contemplatives call infused contemplation or mystical theology. Through this contemplation, God teaches the soul secretly and instructs it in the perfection of love without its doing anything nor understanding how this happens.[378]

The description in Teresa's *Interior Castle* of *acquired recollection* occurs as the night of sense is ending. She indicates that when *infused recollection* occurs, it may be followed by the *Prayer of Quiet* in which the will is absorbed in God even though memory and imagination remain free to wander. Later, as prayer deepens, the imagination and memory will become suspended in the *Prayer of Union*. Ultimately there is the *Prayer of Full Union* in which all the faculties are motionless and rest in God.

It is important to differentiate the *dark nights* from the psychiatric condition of clinical depression.[379] They are quite different phenomena although superficially they may appear similar and sometimes there may indeed be some overlap. A sense of loss is common to both conditions, but it manifests itself differently in each case. In the dark night of sense there is a loss of pleasure, but it lacks the typical mood of clinical depression and other features such as disturbances of appetite and energy. In the dark night of spirit there is acute awareness of faults and imperfections, but they lack the feelings of self-loathing and sometimes suicidal thinking associated with depression. In general, the dark nights in themselves do not produce disorders of eating, sleep, and other physical features such as gastrointestinal upset and chronic pain which are common features of depressive illness. It is noteworthy that Kevin Culligan, a Carmelite spiritual director and counsellor, has reported that his own interior reactions to people in counselling have helped him perceive the difference between depression and the dark nights. He noted that interacting with a depressed person produced in him a feeling of depression. On the other hand, dealing with people going through the dark nights of sense and spirit has seldom led him to such feelings. Instead, he has tended to feel energized as well as having a sense of compassion.[380]

The Carmelite tradition of prayer is thoroughly Christocentric. Both Teresa and John of the Cross also emphasized the Lord's Prayer. Teresa taught that it contains "the entire spiritual way" (WP 42.5).[381] John taught that its seven petitions "embodied everything that is God's will" and that all prayer is "reducible to the Pater Noster" (AC 3.44.4).[382] Focusing on Jesus is the way to the Father and by fixing our eyes only on him "you will discern hidden in him the most secret mysteries, and wisdom, and wonders of God . . . " (AC 2.22.6).[383] For Teresa, prayer was focused on "all our good and help which is the most sacred humanity of our Lord Jesus Christ" (IC 6.7.6).[384] She also stated:

> I am not asking you to do anything more than to look at him. For who can keep you from turning the eyes of your soul towards this Lord, even if you do so just for a moment if you can't do more? ... Your spouse never takes his eyes off you ... In the measure you desire him, you will find him (WP 26.3).[385]

Despite the remarkable contributions of Teresa of Avila and John of the Cross in teaching the ways of prayer, they have both acknowledged that each person's path is unique. Teresa wrote: "God doesn't lead all by one path" (WP 17.2).[386]

Brother Lawrence of the Resurrection

Nicolas Herman, known in religion as Brother Lawrence of the Resurrection, entered the Order of the Discalced Carmelites in Paris as a lay brother in 1640. Prior to becoming a Carmelite, he had done military service in the Thirty Years War and suffered injuries during a siege. He lived a humble life in a Carmelite monastery, serving as a cook and sandal maker. He became very famous and influential through his simple spiritual teaching concerning the practice of the presence of God in the events of ordinary daily life. This "methodless method" involves cultivating awareness of God's presence by periodically turning inward towards him in adoration and love.

Brother Lawrence outlined the process in his *Spiritual Maxims*.[387] He explained in this work the necessity to "keep our eyes fixed on God in everything we say, do, or undertake". Practising the presence of God involves becoming accustomed to his divine company at every moment, particularly at times of suffering or difficulty. During our work and other activities we should "stop for a moment, as often as possible, to adore God in the depths of our hearts, to savour him even though in passing and stealthily". We should do this even when saying vocal prayers. He taught that it is an error for people "not to withdraw from what is external from time to time to adore God within themselves and enjoy his divine presence in peace for a few moments". Adoring God in spirit and truth involves doing so in the depths and centre of our souls.

The practice of the presence of God is the application of our mind to God or remembering him being present. It can be brought about either by the imagination or the understanding. A habit is formed by the repetition of these acts and by frequently bringing the mind back into God's presence. Brother Lawrence taught that "this gentle, loving, awareness of God imperceptibly ignites a divine fire in the soul". To discourage the soul from returning to created things God takes care to provide for it by giving "a very savory, delicious nourishment".

Brother Lawrence advised that we take special care that this inner awareness precedes our activities and accompanies them from time to time. With effort, a habit is formed. Somewhat difficult at first, it draws abundant grace from God and leads to simple awareness of his omnipresence. He described the benefits of the practice as increased faith, hope and love. He mentioned an advanced state of "continual acts of love, adoration, contrition, trust, thanksgiving, oblation, petition, and all the most excellent virtues". He wrote that while few people reach this advanced state which is ultimately a gift, "we can at least acquire, with the help of ordinary grace, a manner and state of prayer that greatly resembles this simple awareness, by means of this practice of the presence of God."[388]

John of Saint Samson

John of Saint Samson (1571–1636), a renowned French Carmelite mystic, was a humble lay brother and an exponent of Prayers of Aspiration. These are essentially acts of love directed to God with few words. He advised that beginners should first gain experience in meditation, cultivating loving conversations with God. Aspirations can then be made at certain intervals. The aspirations gradually become briefer, more concise and they are finally reduced to one word. They can ultimately become a brief, wordless longing. According to Venard Poslusney, "in its highest form it is a simple inclination of the heart, consisting of an intense, burning glance or sigh of love, prolonged for some time."[389]

Prayers of aspiration necessarily include the practice of the presence of God and they fully develop it, extending it with love and desire directed rapidly to God. They can be likened to darts fired into the heavens. They appear to be equivalent to the "arrow prayers" of the Desert Fathers and the "fiery prayer" described by John Cassian. They are prayers made with fervent love, concentrating the heart's affections as far as possible in one word. They may arise as a spontaneous spiritual impulse or they may be a consciously determined raising of the heart to God.

In this chapter, we have noted that in the early years of the Carmelite Order a *lectio divina* pattern of prayer is hinted at in the Rule of Saint Albert. The Carmelite tradition of prayer has always been directed towards contemplation. In their rich spiritual tradition Carmelites have been pre-eminent teachers of the spiritual life and in the ways of prayer. In addition to a brief overview of the teachings of Teresa of Avila and John of the Cross we have also considered the practice of the Presence of God and Prayers of Aspiration. As well as her teachings on meditation and contemplation, Teresa acknowledged the value of verbal prayer said with attentive focus both on the words of prayer and the person to whom it is addressed. Her key emphasis was on prayer as a Christocentric personal encounter with our gaze lovingly directed at Jesus.

CHAPTER 10

The Jesuit Tradition

Ad majorem Dei gloriam
(To the Greater Glory of God)

Jesuit motto

In the sixteenth century Ignatius of Loyola (1491–1556) founded the Society of Jesus (commonly known as the Jesuit Order). This remarkable man made an enormous contribution to the life of the Catholic Church. As pointed out by Cardinal Avery Dulles SJ, "Ignatius stands on the cusp of modernity", representing historically the transition from medieval to modern Catholicism.[390] To appreciate his teachings on prayer, it is at first necessary to consider the story of his life in order to see how the Ignatian methods of prayer are integrated into his spiritual teachings and stem from his personal experiences. While detailed examination of Jesuit tradition is well beyond the scope of this book, it is helpful to focus on the story of the life of Ignatius and some of the key themes recorded in his great work, *The Spiritual Exercises*.

The life of Saint Ignatius of Loyola

Born into a noble family in the Basque region of Spain in 1491, Iñigo de Loyola was an aggressive and arrogant young man in military service in the defence of Navarre, when he was wounded in battle against the French in the siege of Pamplona in 1521.

In later life after his conversion, he changed his name to Ignatius in honour of Ignatius of Antioch, whom he greatly admired. Fighting boldly against impossible odds, he was struck down by enemy fire with a cannonball shattering his right leg. An autobiographical account of his memories was dictated to an early Jesuit scribe Luis Gonçalves da Câmara, who recorded them in a work entitled *Reminiscences*. According to this account: "Until the age of twenty-six he was a man given up to the vanities of the world, and his chief delight used to be in the exercise of arms, with the great and vain desire to gain honor."[391] After his capture he returned to his home country, where he had the agonizing experience of the bones of his leg being reset. Due to subsequent deformity of his leg he voluntarily went through the further ordeal of more surgery to improve his appearance.

While recuperating, he could not gain access to his favourite reading materials consisting of tales of chivalry. So instead he was given a book on the life of Christ and a book on the lives of the saints. He noticed with wonderment that when he read the stories of the saints, he felt consolation and remained happy and content after doing so. In contrast, the romances would give him delight initially, but later they left him feeling dry and dissatisfied. This was the beginning of his experience of "discernment of spirits" in which he would come to know the difference between the "good spirit" from God and the false or "evil spirit". Reflecting on his past life, Ignatius began a conversion experience and resolved that he would do what the saints had done. He formed the wish to go to Jerusalem as a pilgrim and he also contemplated living in penance as a Carthusian monk.

After leaving the castle of Loyola he travelled to the Benedictine monastery of Montserrat where, after an all-night vigil, he left behind his sword and dagger hanging in the church before the altar of the Virgin Mary. Donning the rags of a beggar, he went to the town of Manresa, where he remained for eleven months in a cave as a hermit. During this time, he commenced the meditations and prayers which he later recorded as the *Spiritual Exercises*. During this conversion process he underwent extreme inner sufferings, including obsessional scrupulosity and even the temptation to commit suicide. He noticed great variations in his inner state, sometimes feeling dry and arid in his prayer and at other times feeling the opposite "so suddenly, that it seemed someone had taken away the sadness and the desolation from him like a person taking a cape from someone's shoulders."[392]

He recorded that during this time he would give spiritual assistance to people who came to him. He believed that "at this time God was dealing with him in the same way as a schoolteacher deals with a child, teaching him".[393] One day while sitting by the River Cardoner, he experienced a profound mystical illumination. He reported that his understanding was enlightened so greatly that "it seemed to him as if he were a different person, and he had another mind, different from that which he had before".[394]

In 1523, he left Barcelona to make a pilgrimage to the Holy Land, where he intended to visit the holy places and also engage in a spiritual ministry. When forbidden to remain in Jerusalem, he returned to Spain and began studying Latin, philosophy and theology. He had to endure being investigated by the Inquisition and even had a brief period of imprisonment.

Although exonerated by the Inquisition, he and his early companions faced restrictions on their pastoral ministry. He therefore decided to study at the University of Paris, and in 1534, while there, he and a small group of his early Jesuit companions took vows of poverty and chastity. He had taught his companions the *Spiritual Exercises*, which are a sequential program of meditative reflections and prayer based on Ignatius' own experiences of conversion and the spiritual life. They are conducted with the help of a spiritual director with the aim of helping a person overcome disordered affections and resolve to love and serve God. As he proceeded, Ignatius gave the *Exercises* to many people through personal contact.

With a group of his early companions he travelled to Venice, hoping to subsequently make another pilgrimage to Palestine. They were unable to do so, but Ignatius and five companions were ordained to the priesthood in 1537. Being unable to travel to the Holy Land, Ignatius and his companions then offered their availability to the Pope to serve the Church in any work he directed them to do. Thus there arose a new order, the Society of Jesus, which was a radical innovation at that time, being distinct from the traditional monastic or mendicant orders. They were highly mobile and prepared to live and work anywhere to serve the greater glory of God and work for the good of souls. They were actively involved in the world according to their ideal of finding God in all things.

As pointed out by Avery Dulles, Ignatius was conservative and traditional in many ways, and his ideas reflected Christian feudalism. On the other hand, he was touched by the optimistic spirit of Renaissance humanism. Having a vision of conquering the world for Christ, he was "a spiritual counterpart of the Spanish conquistador".[395]

Jesuits were a major force in the Catholic Counter Reformation, actively recovering some of the losses that had been sustained by the Church of Rome. Throughout its history, the Society of Jesus has exercised a wide-ranging ministry, and has been particularly prominent in the fields of education, missionary activity, pastoral activity, spiritual direction and social justice. Jesuits have remained committed to a deep engagement with the world, in the spirit of being contemplatives in action.

The Spiritual Exercises

The Spiritual Exercises were composed by Ignatius over a number of years. They mirror the journey of his own conversion and the spiritual wisdom gained in the process. They are essentially a handbook for retreat directors, giving practical advice for accompanying and guiding retreatants in meditations and reflections aimed at enabling them to overcome their impediments to loving God and following Christ. The full retreat program envisaged in the *Exercises* is divided into four "weeks", which are not necessarily of exactly seven days duration although the full retreat is envisaged to comprise a total of about thirty days.

The central focus and aim of the *Spiritual Exercises* are expressed in the "Principle and Foundation" taught to the retreatant as a preliminary measure. It states, in part, that:

> The human person is created to praise, reverence and serve God our Lord and by doing so save his or her soul; and it is for the human person that the other things on the face of the earth are created, as helps to the pursuit of this end. It follows from this that the person has to use these things in so far as they help towards this end, and to be free of them in so far as they stand in the way of it . . .

The exercises are designed to elicit direct communication with Christ and increasing degrees of generosity in following him. The theme of the first week is that of conversion from sin and observance of God's commandments. The retreatant focuses on repentance, sin and its consequences, and God's mercy and forgiveness.

Week Two focuses on the call to love and generosity and the following of Christ. During this week, the meditations are centred on the life of Christ up to and including Palm Sunday. Week Three focuses on the Passion of Christ and the desire to grieve with him and Week Four on the joy of Christ's Resurrection.

Ignatius stated that:

> The term 'spiritual exercises' denotes every way of examining one's conscience, of meditating, contemplating, of praying vocally and mentally, and other spiritual activities as will be explained later.[396]

He went on to explain that it is:

> the name given to every way of preparing and making ourselves ready to get rid of all disordered affections so that, once rid of them, one might seek and find the divine will in regard to the disposition of one's life for the salvation of the soul.[397]

In the exercises Ignatius advocated a process which follows a sequence similar to that of the *lectio divina* pattern. The first step involves preliminary prayer followed by meditation on subject matter, either events in the Gospels or other spiritual themes. It is suggested that one enters into the scene being reflected upon by using imaginative images engaging all the senses.

Reflecting and drawing profit from these experiences leads to prayer in the form of what Ignatius called a "colloquy", which is a personal and spontaneous conversation "speaking as one friend speaks with another, or a servant with a master, at times asking for some favour, and other times accusing oneself of something badly done, or sharing personal concerns and asking for advice about them".[398] Each exercise concludes with praying the "Our Father".

Examination of conscience (Examen)

The Examen is another important element of Ignatius' spiritual teachings. The General Examen, which can be usefully performed at the end of the day, contains the following five elements:

1. Giving thanks to God for the favours I have received;
2. Asking for the grace to know my faults and sins and to rid myself of them;
3. Examining in turn my thoughts, words, and deeds which have occurred throughout the day, reviewing the movements of the spirit and my responses;
4. Asking God for forgiveness for my failings and sins;
5. Resolving to respond better henceforth with the help of God's grace. The reflection ends with the praying of the "Our Father".

Ignatius gave the upmost importance to the Examen, and he was never willing to dispense with it. However, it should never be seen solely as a means of behavioural control but should be done out of a desire to co-operate in the work God wishes from us for the service of others.[399]

Discernment of spirits

A central element of Ignatian spirituality is his *Rules for Discernment*.[400] They are divided into two sets of rules, the first set being suitable for the first week of the *Spiritual Exercises* and the second set being more applicable to the second week. Ignatius described them as "Rules by which to perceive and understand to some extent the various movements produced in the soul: the good that they may be accepted, and the bad, they may be rejected."[401]

In his discussion of these rules Ignatius referred to the "good spirit" and the "bad spirit". It should be kept in mind that the concept of good and bad spirits has broader connotations than simply a reference to God and the devil. In essence, it refers broadly to the forces which at any given time incline us either towards or away from God. The Rules grew out of Ignatius' own experience during his process of conversion. From the time he began contrasting the impact of his spiritual reading to that of worldly literature during his convalescence, he became aware that the spirit directing us towards God gives encouragement, strength and consolation on the journey to God, while the bad spirit has a contrary aim and impact.

Ignatius' experience of studying the movements within himself of these opposing forces gave him deep insights and led him to formulate rules to assist in the discernment necessary to discover God's will. In the Ignatian tradition spiritual directors seek to assist people in applying these principles of discernment both when doing the *Spiritual Exercises* in a retreat setting and also more generally when seeking spiritual direction and guidance in their day-to-day lives. This aspect of Ignatian spirituality is outside the scope of this book, but there is no shortage of literature for the interested reader to learn more about the process of discernment.[402]

Three methods of prayer

In his comments for Week Four of the *Spiritual Exercises* Ignatius outlined three ways of praying.[403] The first method is more a preparatory practice than a prayer as such. He recommended meditations on certain spiritual themes, consisting of the Ten Commandments, the deadly sins and contrary virtues, and the powers of the soul and the senses. He stated that this practice "aims more at providing a framework" than being "a method of prayer, properly so-called".[404] The second method of prayer consists of concentrating on the meaning of each word of a prayer. In whatever posture one experiences more devotion, the eyes are closed or fixed on one spot, and attention is held on each word for as long as one finds meaning and consolation in it. If one or two words provide rich material for reflection, relish or consolation there is no rush to proceed further even if a whole hour is spent on those words.

The third method involves praying in synchrony with the rhythm of the breath. One word of a prayer is pronounced between one breath and the next:

> In the interval between each breath attention is especially paid to the meaning of that word, to the person to whom one is praying or to one's lowliness or to the distance between the other's grandeur and one's own lowliness.[405]

CHAPTER 11

Orthodox Teaching on the Jesus Prayer

*For it is the God who said, "Let light shine out of darkness,"
who has shone in our hearts to give the light of the knowledge
of the glory of God in the face of Jesus Christ.*

2 Corinthians 4:6

This chapter provides an overview of Eastern Orthodox teachings about the Jesus Prayer. It will be seen that the views of various Orthodox authorities express consistent understandings about the prayer and its practice. The significance of the Jesus Prayer to Orthodox spirituality is powerfully expressed by the words of Mother Maria of Normanby: "I have come to regard the Jesus Prayer as a mystery of faith. It can neither be comprehended, nor passed on as a particular piece of knowledge. Its essential part cannot be put into words, not because it is too complicated but because it is simple, a thing to be done, directly bound up with the immediate presence of Christ."[406] It should be noted, however, that notwithstanding their great love for this ancient prayer from the Christian East, the Orthodox teachers do not claim that other forms of prayer cannot be equally beneficial. Introducing his discussion of the Jesus Prayer, Metropolitan Kallistos Ware wrote simply that: "One way to embark on this journey inwards is through the Invocation of the Name."[407] Similarly, Fr Lev Gillet indicated the need to avoid a chauvinistic attitude by writing: "The best prayer is for everybody the prayer to which he or she is moved by the Holy Spirit, whatever prayer it may be."[408]

Jesus present in his name

Metropolitan Kallistos has pointed out that the one essential component of the Jesus Prayer is the invocation of the divine name of Jesus.[409] This invocation, however, needs to be done in such a way that it evokes his invisible presence and action. Archimandrite Placide Deseille has likened the repetition of the name to a "verbal icon", leading into the personal presence of Christ. Through his name the divinizing energy of Christ reaches us: "It is a kind of *sacramental*, a sensible reality which is completely penetrated with the acting presence of Christ."[410] Archimandrite Sophrony Sakharov also noted the similarity between the theology of the name and that of the icon. Before the icon of Christ we acknowledge his incarnation, and we go beyond colours and outlines into the world of the spirit. In a similar manner, when we invoke the name we do not elaborate on the sounds but live its content, which remains the same regardless of what language we speak.[411] He emphasized that the invocation of the divine name must involve consciousness of the person of Jesus, whose presence becomes alive and constantly felt within us.[412]

The Orthodox teachers insist that all images and other mental representations are to be excluded at the time of the prayer.[413] The invocation of the name from this perspective is analogous to icons which, although physical depictions, are windows into the invisible spiritual world. They lack the naturalistic, three-dimensional qualities of many other forms of religious art and detail is kept to a minimum. Themes in icons are represented "in a vivid but symbolic, at times abstract, manner".[414] In a similar way, the simple invocation of the name of Jesus with attentive concentration is a window to his presence. From another perspective, Metropolitan Kallistos has also described the Jesus Prayer as a doorway to the "non-iconic" prayer of stillness, free of mental imagery.[415] Placide Deseille has suggested that by the practice of active prayer which is simplified and excluding all discursive activity and imagination, a person can slowly acquire a more profound experience of God.[416]

Although the New Testament attests to the power of the name, Lev Gillet has emphasized that the name is not to be invoked in a merely mechanical manner. He indicated that unless the name both signifies and leads to the presence of Jesus in reality, the invocation would be mere "verbal idolatry".[417] Moreover, it need not be repeated continuously when we are led into periods of mental silence. He used the analogy of a bird beating its wings as it rises into the air, gliding when it has reached the desired height and then only beating its wings from time to time to maintain its flight. He advised that

> the soul having attained to the thought of Jesus and filled herself with the memory of him may discontinue the repetition of the name and rest in the Lord. The repetition will only be resumed when other thoughts threaten to crowd out the thought of Jesus. Then the invocation will start again to gain fresh impetus.[418]

He went on to reflect that:

> This total Presence is all. The name is nothing without the Presence. He who is able constantly to live in the total presence of Our Lord does not need the name. The name is only an incentive to and support to the presence.[419]

Practice of the Jesus Prayer

As noted in chapter 2, the name of Jesus in its Hebrew form denotes God's saving action. Hence in one word it summarizes the whole Gospel. The Jesus Prayer with its repeated cry to the Lord for mercy is therefore both simple and complete. Metropolitan Kallistos has also highlighted its flexibility. As well as variations in the wording, it can be said silently or aloud, alone or in a group setting, at set times or freely at any time.[420]

The Orthodox spiritual masters have offered much practical advice to guide us in praying the Jesus Prayer. They all insist that the prayer is not to be said mechanically but with concentration, compunction and faith. The focus is on the personal presence of Jesus without any visual images or discursive thoughts. The prayer is not an impersonal mantra but an invocation addressed in faith to the person of Jesus. They have all emphasized the importance of approaching the time of prayer with the appropriate attitude and sentiments. These include keeping the commandments, asceticism and humility. Compunction of the heart with repentance for sin is emphasized.[421] Other recommendations have included: spiritual reading or prayers prior to reciting the Jesus Prayer, using a seated posture and choosing a tranquil time and place.[422]

A nineteenth-century Russian Orthodox Bishop, Ignatius Brianchaninov (1807–67), in his writings on the Jesus Prayer stated that he considered it to be a divine institution because of the teaching of Jesus after the mystical supper. He referred to the verses: "I will do whatever you ask in my name, so that the Father may be glorified in the Son. If in my name you ask me anything, I will do it" (John 14:13–14) and "until now you have not asked for anything in my name. Ask and you will receive, so that your joy may be complete" (John 16:24). He taught that while at first the practice of the Jesus Prayer appears dry and unproductive, with perseverance and patience it yields spiritual benefit.[423] He emphasized the need for an experienced spiritual guide to assist us in our practice of the Jesus Prayer[424] and warned that premature striving for advanced contemplative prayer is very harmful.[425] He also taught that the words of the prayer were to be pronounced slowly to allow the mind "time to enter the words as into forms".[426] Although cautioning against the psychophysical methods of the hesychasts, he recognized certain practical aids according to individual needs which can be helpful to beginners. These include: use of a prayer rope, performing prostrations, keeping the eyes closed, praying in a darkened room, and sitting on a low stool, reminiscent of the blind beggar in the Gospel (Mark 10:47).[427] Importantly, he recommended as an absolutely safe method the advice of John Climacus in *The Ladder of Divine Ascent* to "enclose your mind within the words of your prayer" (Step 28). The mind was to stay solely in the words pronounced vocally or mentally and to banish extraneous thoughts. When distracted, one should not be despondent "but remain calm and constantly call your mind back" (Step 4). Praying attentively with the lips, mind and heart, distraction is eventually eliminated with the help of God and constant effort.[428] He further cautioned against reading about advanced prayer without sufficient understanding and pursuing prayer by methods for which one is unready.[429]

Metropolitan Hierotheos Vlachos of Nafpaktos has written of his conversations about the Jesus Prayer with a hermit monk on Mount

Athos.[430] This elder made the observation that once the Jesus Prayer has reached a certain level it gives us rest and calmness and "so even from this point of view it is an invigorating physiological remedy".[431] This interesting phenomenon is illustrated in a description by the author Kyriakos Markides of his meeting with an elderly monk in Cyprus.[432] The ninety-one-year-old monk had been an atheist, never having stepped into a church for fifty-five years, until, at the age of seventy, he had a sudden spiritual conversion. Thereafter he became a monk, devoting the rest of his life to continuous prayer and contemplation. According to Markides, the elder looked at least thirty years younger than his real age, and "he was extraordinarily robust and full of radiant energy."[433] The monk emphasized that his prayer gave him "extraordinary energy and joy".[434]

The vexed question of the role of physical techniques and methods, such as those associated with the hesychasts, has frequently been addressed by the spiritual teachers. Archimandrite Sophrony Sakharov (1896–1993) had been a monk on Mount Athos who later founded the monastery of St John the Baptist at Tolleshunt Knights, Essex, UK. He conceded that the spiritual teachers occasionally permit the use of a technical method of bringing the mind down into the heart, concentration being assisted by linking the first part of the prayer with inhalation of the breath and the second part with exhalation. Nonetheless, he taught that true prayer comes through faith and repentance and there is danger in attributing too much significance to methodology. His concerns about excessive reliance on methodology mirror the teachings of Ignatius Brianchaninov, who also cautioned against psychophysical methods, pointing out that they were merely aids and could lead to a wrong materialistic concept of prayer rather than true spiritual understanding.[435]

Fr Sophrony recommended fixing attention on the name of Jesus Christ and the words of the prayer. Then at a certain stage the mind naturally follows the heart. He pointed out that if the prayer were detached from the person of Jesus and reduced to a technical exercise, it would contravene the commandment against taking the name of the Lord in vain.[436] He emphasized the need for continuing ascetic struggle and observance of the commandments, and warned against trying to force our spiritual progress to hurry the process.[437] He taught that humility and repentance are paramount and through experiencing the ebb and flow of God's grace we learn the need to be poor in spirit. Thus, when we find God no longer with us, we cry out to him with repentance.[438]

Although John Climacus may not have been describing the modern form of the Jesus Prayer, his *Ladder of Divine Ascent* taught practices very relevant to the Jesus Prayer. In Step 21 he urged the invocation of the divine name: "Flog your enemies with the name of Jesus, since there is no stronger weapon in heaven or on earth."[439] In Step 27 the wording suggests linkage of the rhythm of the breath to the invocation to Jesus: "Let the remembrance of Jesus be present with your every breath. Then indeed you will appreciate the value of stillness."[440] He advocated a method of focused concentration: "Make the effort to raise up, or rather, to enclose your mind within the words of your prayer; and if like a child, it gets tired and falters, raise it up again" (Step 28).[441] Dealing with recurring distractions is addressed in Step 4: "Do not lose heart when your thoughts are stolen away. Just remain calm, and constantly call your mind back."[442]

In modern times many people practise the Jesus Prayer without affiliation to a Church. This reflects the historical trajectory of the Jesus Prayer, which has become increasingly more widely known beyond the formal boundaries of the Eastern Orthodox Churches. As a result, for some the context of the Jesus Prayer with its original liturgical and sacramental setting within a Church community has been attenuated or lost. The risk is that for many the practice of the Jesus Prayer can become "privatized" and isolated from the broader tradition that can support, guide and nurture a person's progress on the spiritual path. While good in itself, the Jesus Prayer should not be practised in isolation from a spiritual family and support from the other sources of grace. As noted by Metropolitan Kallistos, such a situation is anomalous.[443]

Progress in the Jesus Prayer

The Jesus Prayer is ultimately a means of realizing within ourselves the mystery of *theosis*.[444] Fr Placide Deseille has described progress in prayer as a movement from a series of acts to a state of being. The active phase of conscious effort involves vocal prayer, which becomes progressively simplified to finally arrive at truly contemplative prayer. Although not absolutely mutually exclusive, two stages can be identified. Firstly, a person actively engages in the spiritual life, seeking unity with God. Then there is a second stage in which God intervenes more actively with his gifts of grace.[445] Fr Placide wrote that the Eastern tradition stresses that vocal prayer in the first phase is to be said with concentration, without engaging in discursive reflections.[446] Hence he described the Jesus Prayer as producing a certain impoverishment of the discursive intellect, greatly simplifying mental and intellectual activity. He taught that contemporary spiritual Fathers consider it sufficient to say the prayer slowly, calmly, in accordance with the pattern of one's breathing, enclosing oneself in the spirit of the words. He wrote: "It is as if one were seated before the Lord, like a beggar or supplicant at the side of the road, and crying out one's desire, one's appeal to passers-by from time to time."[447] While prayed intermittently, its purpose is to conduct us to a state of continual prayer.[448]

Metropolitan Kallistos also referred to the progression over time through the levels of oral prayer, mental prayer and prayer of intellect-in-the-heart. With the help of God's grace, the prayer becomes more inward, pervasive and ultimately, self-acting. Such prayer usually comes only after a very long period of spiritual struggle and asceticism and if it occurs, it is always the free gift of God.[449]

A notable contribution to Orthodox teaching about the Jesus Prayer was made by Russian Orthodox Archbishop Anthony Golynsky-Mihailovsky (1889–1977), who had suffered terrible persecution in Soviet Russia. He was arrested by the KGB, experienced torture and served terms of imprisonment in concentration camps. Following his last term of imprisonment from 1950 until 1956, he spent the remaining twenty years of his life devoted to his spiritual children. His ministry had to be carried out secretly to avoid arrest. At the request of his spiritual children, Archbishop Anthony wrote notes which were later published, giving practical guidelines for praying the Jesus Prayer.[450] Unlike many other writings on the Jesus Prayer, which have focused on advanced levels of mystical prayer, he concentrated on advice for beginners. He emphasized that progress in the prayer starts with human effort in the active stage and later proceeds towards contemplation where divine grace ultimately takes over.

He gave detailed teachings about three forms of the prayer accessible through active effort, encompassing the progression of the prayer from verbal, to mental, to mind-in-the-heart with increasing surrender to the will of God. He also described further kinds of more advanced prayer, which become self-acting and associated with purification from passions and sin. Truly contemplative prayer leads into the highest gift of visionary prayer (*theoria*). The path involves struggle and spiritual warfare. He emphasized the need for an experienced teacher if possible, and stressed the great importance of frequency of prayer.[451] No verbal or mental images were to be accepted.[452] In common with other Orthodox teachers, Archbishop Anthony emphasized repentance and mourning over one's sinfulness and cautioned against trying to force progress. He had much less to say about the higher levels of prayer. He recognized that the experience of visionary prayer (*theoria*) is an ineffable state.[453] Fr Sophrony Sakharov described the same progression from verbal to mental, then to mind-in-the-heart, followed by self-acting prayer, and finally a state of spiritual contemplation. The time taken depends on the intensity of repentance.[454]

Conclusions

The brief review of the teachings of the Orthodox authorities discussed in this chapter allows us to discern common principles concerning the practice of the Jesus Prayer. In relation to prayer in general, the spiritual teachers of both the East and West recognize that the path of deepening union with God in prayer involves a progression from an active process involving human effort to one in which a person increasingly surrenders to God's action of grace manifested in contemplative prayer. The path to contemplation involves an interior movement of consciousness into the depths of one's heart and soul. In both traditions, repentance, humility and ascetic struggle against sin and evil are considered essential. Both traditions emphasize the need to avoid striving to acquire those spiritual experiences which can only be received as a free gift from God. The Orthodox teachers of the Jesus Prayer allow some flexibility in the wording of the prayer itself but insist on the essential requirement that there be an invocation of the divine name of Jesus. The prayer focuses on the presence of Jesus, who is addressed personally with faith, love and devotion. The attitude should be like that of the blind beggar in the Gospel who pleads for God's mercy (Mark 10:46–52). The prayer is not practised mechanically like an impersonal mantra. Concentration on the words of the prayer is recommended and all discursive thoughts, imagination, fantasy and imagery are to be avoided. While caution is advised in the use of elaborate psychophysical methods, simple aids such as use of a prayer rope and a suitable seated posture are encouraged. Wherever possible, the Jesus Prayer should be practised under the guidance of a suitably experienced spiritual teacher. Perseverance is necessary as it is recognized that initially, conscious effort and much ascetic struggle is required in practising the Jesus Prayer.

Many excellent books have been written about the Jesus Prayer. In addition to the books by Metropolitan Kallistos Ware previously referenced in this chapter, there is a very useful text written by Orthodox writer Frederica Mathewes-Green.[455] There are also books written by Anglican Bishop Simon Barrington-Ward, which focus on praying the Jesus Prayer in a group setting.[456] Two other works which provide rich reflections on the spirituality and practice of the Jesus Prayer are *On the Invocation of the Name of Jesus* written by Lev Gillet and *Prayer of the Heart* by George Maloney.[457]

CHAPTER 12

Precautions and Controversies

*Beloved, do not believe every spirit, but test the
spirits to see whether they are from God.*
1 John 4:1

Test everything; hold fast to what is good.
1 Thessalonians 5:21

Let us pause for reflection on some words of caution and several issues in dispute. All the great teachers of both the Eastern and Western Churches warn about the potential dangers on the spiritual path. In this chapter we consider some of their warnings.

A cautionary tale

There is a tale from the Talmud concerning four masters entering "The Garden of Delight".[458] The first to enter this mystical realm was ben Azai, who looked around there and died. To him was applied the verse of Scripture: "Precious in the sight of the Lord is the death of his faithful ones" (Psalm 116:15). The second master, ben Zoma, looked around, lost his reason and became insane. The third master, Aher, who had reputedly been one of the wisest teachers in Israel, abandoned his moral principles. He became an apostate, leading a scandalous life of immorality, and even became implicated in the murder of a child. Finally, the great Rabbi Akiba entered the garden in peace and came out in peace.

This allegory is highly relevant to our topic as it highlights the dangers of being prematurely exposed to deeper levels of consciousness or higher psychic or spiritual experiences without having the appropriate capacity or being properly prepared and strengthened through asceticism and moral strength. God does not wish us to have experiences which are too overwhelming and beyond our ability to deal with appropriately.

Virtue and ascetic struggle

The story of the four masters suggests that the potential dangers can be physical, psychological or spiritual. It is in this context that we must view Teresa of Avila's teaching on the need for love, humility, detachment and determination as preparatory and indispensable qualities needed for achieving our full potential in spiritual transformation. Similarly, we must accept the teachings of the Orthodox masters about the essential need for the ascetic struggle, which includes repentance and humility. We need to take to heart the very clear warnings of all the Orthodox teachers mentioned in chapter 11 concerning the risks of premature striving for the advanced spiritual states which are given only as God's free gift. Such experiences are revealed in due course when God accepts our repentance. These teachers have stressed the importance of having direction and guidance from an experienced elder to reduce the risk of becoming carried away with pride in response to spiritual experiences.

A major concern of the Orthodox teachers is the danger of spiritual deception or illusion known by the Russian term *prelest* (in Greek: *planē*). The most spectacular form of this disorder is when a person strives for a higher spiritual state or exalted religious feelings without being purified of passions. The deluded person is the victim of an inflated ego, pride and self-deception. In this state the difference between the grace of God and its counterfeit cannot be discerned.[459] The Orthodox tradition has always recognized the necessity for intense spiritual warfare to gain purification, victory over passions and selfishness. It has also stipulated the acquisition of repentance and humility as essential preparations to receive God's grace. Bearing in mind the warnings of these spiritual teachers, we need to be aware of the susceptibility which we all have to conceit and pride. We should recall that even Paul's famous "thorn in the flesh" was allowed by God to prevent him from becoming too elated by his profound mystical experiences (2 Corinthians 12:7).

Physical techniques

Another basis for caution relates to the use of methodologies derived from non-Christian Eastern traditions. The psychophysical methods of the hesychasts can also be misinterpreted, leading to a materialistic understanding of contemplative prayer. Moreover, interfering with one's breathing patterns or heartbeats can potentially cause serious physical or mental harm. Anything more than simply letting the words of the prayer synchronize with the ebb and flow of the breath may be damaging and should therefore be avoided on that basis alone. If undertaken at all, these physical methods should be done only under the guidance of a spiritual director suitably experienced in practising the Jesus Prayer.

Using physical techniques can lead to thinking of prayer as something acquired mechanically through natural means. Material aids to prayer are on no account to be confused with the actual operation of prayer itself. They are mere accessories to assist our weakness but undue reliance on them is dangerous. Obeying the commandments, practising the prayer attentively and maintaining repentance leads to Prayer of the Heart and avoids the dangers of delusion.

Meditation and mantras

A very important matter is the question of how Meditation and the influence of non-Christian Eastern religions relate to Christian prayer. As discussed in chapter 4, the historical development of the Jesus Prayer can be traced to the Desert Fathers. In their quest for constant remembrance of God in unceasing prayer, the Fathers developed a practice of short phrases, "monologistic" or "arrow prayers", to obviate distractions and focus concentration. The monastic culture which the Jesus Prayer arose from the fourth and fifth centuries onwards emphasized worship and prayer with psalmody through which Christ was persistently invoked.[460]

As we have noted previously, Cassian was an important influence on Benedict, who recommended to his monks that they read his works. We have also noted in chapter 7 that in studying Cassian's *Conference 10* John Main saw in its description the characteristics of a *mantra*, thereby believing that he had discovered in the Christian tradition a method of Meditation and contemplative prayer consistent with that which he had learnt from the Hindu teacher. He also considered that there were elements of the same mantra tradition in Western Christian spirituality in the writings of the author of *The Cloud of Unknowing*. Although these interpretations may be questioned, nevertheless the writings of Cassian inspired John Main to develop his mantra style of Christian Meditation. The popularity of this development is witnessed by the worldwide proliferation of numerous Christian Meditation Centres throughout the world. We have also noted in chapter 8 that there is reason to question whether the practice of Centering Prayer can be said to fully represent the teachings of *The Cloud of Unknowing*.

A terminological issue concerns the meaning of the word "mantra". This question is somewhat confusing, because this word has now passed into common language to indicate the use of a repetitive phrase of some sort, not necessarily having any religious significance. Moreover, because of the connotations of Hinduism with its various usages of mantras, it is perhaps unfortunate that John Main felt the need to use the term in his description of Christian Meditation, thereby suggesting in the eyes of some, the undue influence of non-Christian or alien traditions. It is difficult, however, to think of an alternative term for what is in fact a mantra used for a concentrative style of Meditation, albeit one adapted for use as a Christian spiritual practice. In English, Cassian's word "formula" conveys a different sense and in fact, as previously discussed, it is not identical to a mantra.

In the discussion of Indian mantras in this book it was noted that in Hinduism, mantras are associated with ritualistic worship and various essentially "magical" and occult practices. They are also claimed to represent the power or presence of various deities of the Hindu pantheon. In addition, there are beliefs that the actual vibrational qualities of the sounds of mantras are efficacious. The Yoga Sutras of Patañjali suggest that the repetitions of a mantra and focus on its meaning can overcome distractions and promote inner concentration. The mantra as used in Christian Meditation does not aim to possess Hindu qualities, but it is used purely as a psychological instrument to focus and stabilize the mind and produce concentration and inwardness. There is some research evidence that the efficacy of mantra Meditation as indicated by physiological or psychosocial outcome measures may not depend on what actual mantra is chosen. This evidence supports the idea that the key ingredient in Meditation may be the use of a mental device, whether or not it is a mantra that acts as a focus of attention.[461]

Despite his contact with a Hindu Swami, John Main maintained his Christian faith, and he later became a Benedictine monk. He advised that for Christian Meditation the mantra should be a word within Christian tradition. He recommended *"Maranatha"*, a word mentioned in the New Testament. His concept of mantra stripped it of non-Christian connotations. Instead, it is seen merely as a device for detaching from our own thoughts and turning our attention beyond ourselves and towards God. The idea was that in bypassing conscious, discursive mental functioning one reached deeper levels of consciousness, and ultimately silence.

It has sometimes also been claimed that the Jesus Prayer itself is a mantra, a suggestion rightly contested by Orthodox authorities. It is reasonable to describe it as having a mantra-like characteristic in the sense of involving a repetitive invocation. The repetitions have the effect of reducing distraction and assisting with concentration. However, the Jesus Prayer differs greatly from any non-Christian prayer or mantra-based Meditation. It is a direct invocation to the person of Jesus, expressing faith in his divinity and a plea for his mercy. It does not just rely upon mechanical technique and is not in the nature of a magical incantation. Its efficacy is the result of God's grace, freely given. It is not an impersonal instrument but a prayer replete with meaning, expressing sentiments of humility, repentance, compunction and love. It is a cataphatic prayer which by God's grace may progress to an apophatic prayer of inner stillness.

In contrast, Christian Meditation uses a mantra which is not a prayer in itself or a direct, personal invocation, but is used instrumentally to bypass thinking and imagery. The meditator is told not to think about the actual *meaning* of the mantra at the time of meditation, even though the word itself may have intrinsic Christian significance. There is little doubt that John Main viewed contemplative prayer as a simple reaching out to God, and in Christian Meditation he did so with Christian faith. Christian Meditation, although profoundly simple, is also more rigidly structured than the Jesus Prayer, which has significant flexibility and much theological richness in its wording.

Meditation and prayer

A central question is whether practices such as Christian Meditation or Centering Prayer constitute specifically Christian prayer. A group of sixteen people associated with Christian Meditation at *Unitas*, a centre founded by John Main, responded to a series of questions about this Meditation practice.[462] In response to the question of what makes mantra Meditation specifically Christian it was suggested that the "Christian-ness" of the prayer was contained in the *intention* of the meditator, the Christian faith that is brought to the practice. While the intention is not consciously dwelt upon during the period of meditation itself, it is formulated in the meditator's daily Christian life. Meditation can be either discursive (involving thinking, reasoning, imagining, remembering and feeling) or non-discursive, in which the mental activities are quiet in order to be silent and passive before God and receptive to whatever he wishes to communicate to us. Although non-discursive Meditation does not constitute infused contemplation, it disposes the meditator to receive the grace of contemplation which is ultimately God's free gift. Noting that many Christians report never being able to pray discursively, it was considered that they could begin interior prayer with non-discursive Meditation, provided their knowledge and love of God was being nourished through other sources, such as spiritual reading or liturgical worship.[463]

Despite their widespread appeal, attempts to introduce methods derived from Eastern religions and traditions into Christian prayer have not been without criticisms. One critic of Christian Meditation, for example, has expressed concerns about the prospect of altered states of consciousness, susceptibility to demonic influences and the experiences referred to in Hinduism as "the awakening of kundalini".[464] The mere fact that practices such as Meditation can sometimes precipitate psychological disturbances is hardly surprising. It is well known that even simple relaxation techniques can occasionally produce paradoxical reactions, such as panic attacks and other disturbances in vulnerable individuals.

This issue raises the question of appropriate preparation, screening measures and support for people susceptible to negative effects from Meditation. The fact that Christian Meditation is now practised internationally and supported by many Catholic authorities suggests that it has been widely perceived as positive and beneficial rather than problematic.

Centering Prayer has also attracted criticism for reasons similar to those raised against Christian Meditation. One trenchant critic has outlined various ways in which the teachings of Thomas Keating diverge from those of Teresa of Avila.[465] These include the contrast between the practice of letting go of thoughts in Centering Prayer and Teresa's advice to continue using our mental faculties unless God suspends them with infused contemplation.

Related to the criticisms of the practices of both Christian Meditation and Centering Prayer and their acceptability as Christian forms of prayer is the problem of the transition from active (cataphatic) prayer to mystical (apophatic) prayer, which is essentially a passive receptivity to God's grace. In the former category are prayers involving words and concepts whereas the latter involves ineffable experiences which, according to the teachings of Teresa of Avila and John of the Cross, are free gifts from God which cannot be acquired by any method or technique on our part. The question arises as to what a person should do if they reach a situation in which they feel dryness or inability to engage in the traditional discursive meditation and prayer practices. The fact that there were so many people in this category was a major impetus to the drive to introduce into Christian prayer methods derived from non-Christian Eastern practices. The fact that these practices have flourished indicates that they are meeting a perceived need felt by many. They can easily become ways of trying to actively achieve contemplation. We are then confronted with the question of whether there is such a thing as acquired contemplation. Grappling with that issue has been a vexed question apparent in the Church of the West since the time of Teresa of Avila and John of the Cross.

Between meditation and contemplation

For John of the Cross contemplation meant infused contemplation, an actual experience of God's presence and grace. It is clearly differentiated from ordinary prayers which we can make by our own efforts such as verbal prayer, discursive forms of meditation, practice of the presence of God, and aspirational prayers. In practice there is a transitional zone in which a person starts to experience signs of the call to contemplation. The onset of this transition is heralded at first by a sense of dryness and aridity associated with the dark night of the senses. The person is drawn to being alone with a general loving awareness of God. This experience enables a person to progress from discursive meditations in favour of a more simplified, affective form of prayer consisting of a loving gaze and focus on the presence of God.

James Arraj has drawn attention to the problems associated with the notion of acquired contemplation. He has argued that this notion is a misinterpretation of the teachings of John of the Cross.[466] For John, contemplation does not come through the natural activity of the faculties. As noted by Arraj, the dark night of sense heralds the beginning of contemplation, an inner quiet which is

> a loving knowledge that comes, not through the faculties of sense, imagination, intellect, memory or will, but wells up from the depths of the heart and draws us into those depths, to rest there and receive what God is giving us.[467]

At this stage a person "must be content simply with a loving and peaceful attentiveness to God" and abandon desires and discursive meditations (DN 1.10.4).[468] We have noted in chapter 9 that Teresa described two kinds of prayers of recollection which precede the Prayer of Quiet. One is an active process of *acquired recollection*. Teresa calls it recollection "because the soul collects together all the faculties and enters within itself to be with its God. Its Divine Master comes more speedily to teach it, and to grant it the Prayer of Quiet, than in any other way" (WP 28).[469]

The other form of recollection is passive and supernatural, and "it doesn't come when we want it but when God wants to grant us this favour" (IC 4.3.3).[470] Teresa clearly taught that we should not try to suspend our cognitive processes prior to God drawing us beyond them. Her comments are interesting:

> This recollection is a preparation for being able to listen, as is counselled in some books, so that the soul instead of striving to engage in discourse strives to remain attentive and aware of what the Lord is working in it. If His Majesty has not begun to absorb us, I cannot understand how the mind can be stopped. There is no way of doing so without bringing about more harm than good, although there has been a lengthy controversy on this matter among some spiritual persons (IC 4.3.4).[471]

She goes on to write:

> If we don't yet know whether this King has heard or seen us, we must not become fools. The soul does become quite a fool when it tries to induce this prayer, and it is left much drier; and the imagination perhaps becomes more restless through the effort made not to think of anything (IC 4.3.5).[472]

Furthermore, she advises:

> Since God gave us our faculties that we might work with them and in this work they find their reward, there is no reason to charm them; we should let them perform their task until God appoints them to another greater one (IC 4.3.6).[473]

As outlined in chapter 11, the Orthodox teachers of the Jesus Prayer give the same message as Teresa on this matter. The words of the prayer are to be repeatedly and attentively addressed to the person of Jesus without premature striving for spiritual experiences. Progress to the deeper levels of prayer cannot be forced and only occurs under the guidance of God's grace when he wishes to confer such gifts.

Arraj has commented further on the recurring problem of the transition from meditation to contemplation resulting in people feeling pressured to seek an answer in the direction of acquired contemplation. This is a response to the issue of what to do when we cannot meditate like we used to, but we have not yet received the beginnings of infused contemplation. He has cautioned that we should not "give in to the understandable impulse to replace infused contemplation with a host of active or acquired contemplations, so that in some way we can call ourselves contemplatives."[474]

Arraj has suggested the concept of "the spiritual unconscious" as a framework to understand what to do with our natural faculties when we find ourselves entering the dark night of sense.[475] He draws on the idea of mystical experience as "an experimental knowledge of the deep things of God", which comes through faith.[476] The foundation of this knowledge is the indwelling of God in our souls by grace, and mystical experience is knowledge that comes through a loving union with God. Gifts of the Holy Spirit dispose us to mystical experience. In the depths of the human spirit we obtain and continue to receive our existence from God. Arraj has noted that our faculties are only remote means of drawing into deep union with God. The intellect still operates in its limited, discursive way, so only faith combined with love and gifts of the Holy Spirit can lead to divine union. The transformation that is involved appears to us as suffering and death. In responding to the call to infused contemplation, the faculties fail.

Arraj considered that divine union is rooted in the depths of the spiritual unconscious and if we are being drawn into the depths "we must allow this to happen and meet this loving presence with our own loving attentiveness and receptivity. If we are not being drawn into those depths, we cannot abandon the work of the faculties."[477] Divine union cannot be acquired by anything we do and we can only prepare ourselves to receive it if it comes; if it does not, we are to continue loving God as much as possible. Arraj suggested that we should often lessen the activity of our faculties and devote ourselves to loving God and being in his presence in faith. This involves active, loving attentiveness and receptivity to God, but this simplification of prayer must be carefully distinguished from imagining we can bridge the gap between our active faculties and the passive reception of contemplation. He warned that if the lessening of our active faculties goes too far, it can leave us in a void with no guarantee that it is a prelude to infused contemplation. He viewed the growing life of grace and love as coming from the depths but making itself felt in consciousness.

As the faculties become progressively less prominent, a general loving knowledge of God gains expression in consciousness. Arraj noted that if for some reason this knowledge recedes back into the depths of the spiritual unconscious, the advice of John of the Cross is that we should return to the working of the faculties. Neither acts of the faculties nor attempts to stop their working can produce contemplation.[478]

Imagery and prayer

An issue of significance is the contrasting attitudes between the Ignatian tradition on the one hand and the Eastern Orthodox teachers on the other, with regard to the place of imagery and imagination in prayer. As outlined in chapter 10, the *Spiritual Exercises* emphasized imaginative meditations on spiritual themes and incidents from the Gospels. This differs from the Jesus Prayer, where imagery is eschewed and instead the focus of attention is confined to the brief words of the prayer and a sense of the presence of Jesus. The concerns of the Orthodox teachers are understandable in that being drawn into fantasy can provide images which constitute a barrier to immediate and authentic face to face contact with Christ. Engagements with fantasy images may also present a risk for persons with psychological vulnerabilities or proneness to mental instability. It would seem to be wise advice to avoid imagination and imagery during the actual time of prayer. On the other hand, it must be recognized that the *Spiritual Exercises* of Ignatius of Loyola, in which imagery is employed, are themselves not simply prayer but a more complex process of thinking, imagination, and reflection, including preparation for prayer. To that extent, they are not strictly comparable to the Jesus Prayer.

Although the use of imagery is the most widely known feature of the Ignatian prayer tradition, it is noteworthy that Ignatius himself was aware that there are others forms of efficacious prayer. His recognition of the need to address varied individual requirements is reflected in his mention of two other methods of prayer: viz, concentrated focus on the actual words of the prayer, and prayer said in synchrony with the breathing rhythm. As has been discussed in this book, both of these methods are widely used in the practice of the Jesus Prayer.

"Creative illness"

The allegorical tale of the four masters illustrates the potential traumas on the spiritual journey. Profound transformation involves a process of purification and repentance. This inevitably includes suffering and trials. An historical example is the story of Ignatius Loyola himself. In his biographical study of Ignatius, Jesuit priest and psychiatrist William Meissner has outlined from a psychoanalytic perspective the enormous suffering undergone by Ignatius during his conversion because of the inner trauma involved in such a radical and extreme transformation from arrogant, narcissistic hidalgo into the humble pilgrim and man of God.[479] Presumably the degree of suffering reflects the amount of purification involved.

A modern example of the phenomenon of spiritual suffering is that of Irish-born Jesuit William Johnston (1925–2010) who was a prominent authority on spirituality and mysticism. In his autobiography he described a five-year period in which he suffered a range of disturbing symptoms arising from the depths of his unconscious. These included inexplicable fears, anxiety and panic, a disturbing inability to sleep and sensory disturbances with hallucinatory features. He consulted various people and a psychiatrist friend about this matter. It was recognized that he was not experiencing a conventional psychological illness and he eventually came to understand this experience as being the inner fire of purification, to which there was no solution except patient endurance to let the process unfold. He noted that this is a frequent occurrence in spiritual and prayerful people who are often wrongly characterized as being "sick". He also noted that although John of the Cross had described such an experience poetically in terms of the living flame of love tenderly wounding his soul in its deepest centre, John had also harkened back to an earlier time when the flame was experienced as oppressive.[480]

In the Hindu tradition such phenomena are usually interpreted in terms of the notion of *kundalini*, an energy said to be associated with spiritual awakening. Many Christians have considered this to be a demonic force, but Philip St. Romain in his study of this phenomenon considers it to be a natural life energy that can be aroused in various ways or even occur spontaneously.[481] He considers it likely that it has been experienced by a number of Christian mystics, such as Teresa of Avila, who have understood it as representing a deepening union with God. While it has been described in a way that seems alien to the Christian worldview, he believes that a Christian philosophical and theological explanation for it will eventually be developed. However these phenomena may be interpreted, there is little doubt about the reality of such disturbances which may not be uncommon in people pursuing the spiritual life. The dangers on the path highlight the importance of obtaining guidance whenever possible from a wise and holy spiritual father as a protective factor. The story of the four masters at the start of this chapter is highly instructive.

From a psychoanalytic perspective periods of emotional disturbance have sometimes been seen as "creative illness".[482] Such states have also been considered to be "spiritual emergency" and differentiated from psychiatric disorders.[483] Given the nature of these phenomena, it is folly for anyone to try to induce spiritual experiences or presume to force spiritual progress. The only appropriate stance is to persevere with prayer, serving God as best we can, and leaving it to him to give us his support and grace as and when he sees our need.

Spiritual discernment

Another issue which both the Eastern and Western teachers discuss is the question of the subjective interpretation of our psychological or spiritual experiences. It is commonly agreed that feelings of sweetness and bliss as well as more spectacular psychic phenomena are not to be seen as indicators of saintliness or great virtue. They may indeed not be communications from God but rather, in the words of Ignatius, from the "bad spirit" disguised as an angel of light. In these circumstances we can be easily misled into responding inappropriately and becoming puffed up with pride at our imagined spiritual superiority. In other words, our experiences must be subject to discernment.

The contribution of Ignatius of Loyola is relevant here, because his *Rules for Discernment* were written precisely to assist people to develop greater capacity for self-knowledge and to discover God's will in their day-to-day lives. We can be assisted by teachings such as the *Rules for Discernment* or feedback from a spiritual director. Fundamentally, the ultimate indicators are the fruits of our experiences, such as whether they lead to greater humility, patience, tolerance and love for others in our day-to-day lives. Given that good feelings per se are not a reliable guide, we may wonder about the purpose of such spiritual feelings and consolations. Teresa of Avila assists us here in her observation that such favours are meant to strengthen, nourish and sustain us for the journey ahead where there will no doubt be further trials and difficulties. Ignatius of Loyola also sheds light on this issue in his *Rules for Discernment*, in which he advised that when experiencing spiritual consolations, we should utilize them with a view to future desolate times, and so store up these good memories and strength for the challenges to come.[484]

Orthodox perspectives

From an Orthodox perspective there are likely to be reservations concerning practices such as Christian Meditation or Centering Prayer. Christian Orthodoxy would reject as unacceptable anything suggestive of "New Age" practices, Hindu (or other non-Christian) practices, syncretism, or occult phenomena. John Main's use of a "mantra", although removed from its Hindu context, would possibly be looked upon with suspicion. Some Orthodox authors have written harrowing accounts of dabbling in non-Christian Eastern religions.[485] Such accounts often detail occurrences of disturbing encounters with occultism and demonic forces until the authors subsequently find deliverance within Orthodoxy.[486]

Seraphim Rose (1934–82) strongly criticized the spread into Christianity of ideas and practices from Eastern religions. He stated that: "These movements have no foundations in Christian tradition or practice but are purely the product of Eastern pagan religions and of modern spiritism, more or less diluted and often presented as 'nonreligious.'" He considered that such practices were an entrance into the "cosmic" spiritual realm of demons. He saw this as producing a false Christian "spirituality".[487] The Greek text of Psalm 95:5 (LXX) has been translated in the *Orthodox Study Bible* as: "For all the gods of the nations are demons."[488] The Hebrew text uses the word "idols" (*elilim*) in contrast to "demons" (*daimonia*) in the Greek. It is therefore understandable that for the Orthodox the use of a mantra, however modified, would raise concerns about non-Christian influences and susceptibility to phenomena such as contact with occult powers and demonic spirits.[489]

Notwithstanding these concerns it might be argued that as used in Christian Meditation the mantra is a purely natural psychological tool which is as innocuous as certain postures or gestures commonly used to assist in Christian prayer. Furthermore, the likely historical interactions between Sufism and hesychasm with the use of psychophysical techniques similar to those used in Hindu yoga tends to undercut objections coming from the Orthodox perspective. Even though these techniques were very much in the nature of secondary aids to assist concentration and prayer, the fact remains that such methods from non-Christian sources appear to have been incorporated, albeit very peripherally, into an Orthodox practice.

Personal encounter with Christ

A related issue concerns the impersonal aspect of the mantra used in Christian Meditation, in contrast to the direct, *personal* invocation in the Jesus Prayer. The apparent short-circuiting of cataphatic prayer by means of a mantra to achieve the silence of apophatic prayer is also noteworthy. In the light of the teachings of Fr Sophrony Sakharov in our discussion in chapter 11, and the criticism of Bourgeault, the impersonal quality of the mantra in Christian Meditation appears problematic. Although the Meditation is entered into with Christian faith oriented towards God, the element of personal invocation and relationship with Christ characteristic of cataphatic Christian prayer is not explicitly expressed. Given that its invocation is a personal communication with Christ, the Jesus Prayer obviously avoids any such difficulty.

Centering Prayer differs from Christian Meditation in its use of a sacred word in that the word is not continually repeated like a mantra, but it is only used as a way of returning the person to the condition of reaching out to God. This form of prayer also lacks an explicit invocation to Christ. The claim that it has significant benefits in terms of psychological healing, if correct, is a significant and positive feature. In those circumstances, however, there is the potential for it to be used merely as a method of psychological therapy rather than being practised as a true prayer. The use of a short word such as "God" or "love" as envisaged by the author of *The Cloud of Unknowing* really represents an aspirational "arrow prayer" directed with love by a person responding to the first stirrings of the call to contemplation. The sacred word in Centering Prayer appears to be used in a more detached manner, symbolizing an intention to consent to God rather that carrying the intensity of devotional feeling of the chosen word as described in *The Cloud*.

Writing about the crucial issue of the place of Christ in Christian mysticism, William Johnston has considered the question of the place of Christ the Incarnate Word in contemplative prayer practices. He posed the question: "But how does Christ the man fit into this imageless, supra-conceptual void? Where is Christ when I am between the cloud of unknowing and the cloud of forgetting?"[490] He suggested a way towards a possible solution to this dilemma by pointing out that the Christian prays not just to the historical figure of Jesus but to the risen Christ. Christ in both his historical and his risen existence is the same Jesus, but the mode of his existence is quite different. While we can have thoughts and images of the historical Jesus, we can have no adequate image of the transcendent cosmic Christ, whom we seek in prayer. Hence, ineffable apophatic prayer can still be thoroughly Christocentric.[491]

In writing about the Jesus Prayer, Fr Sophrony Sakharov emphasized the fact that God has revealed himself to Moses as *personal* and the one true *being*, I AM.[492] Subsequent revelations have disclosed his attributes as merciful and the lover of mankind.[493] The name Jesus, meaning "God the Saviour", was a name given to many other men, but we utter it in prayer in another "frame" of spirit. In that context, God is present in this name "like a scent-flask full of fragrance", conveying divine energy. In our invocation of the divine names we do not attribute to them magic powers due to their sounds. Instead, they are pronounced as a true confession of faith in a state of awe, reverence and love.[494]

As a young man Fr Sophrony himself had engaged in Buddhist practices for a time before returning to Orthodoxy. He considered it most unacceptable to identify the Jesus Prayer as akin to yoga, Buddhism, "Transcendental Meditation" and the like. The difference is that these other paths deflect our mind from a personal relationship with God to an abstract, transpersonal absolute and an impersonal asceticism. He conceded that in diverting our mind from imagery, "meditation can afford us a sense of tranquillity, of peace, a release from time and space but there is no feeling of standing before a personal God. It is not real prayer face-to-Face."[495]

To meditate can mean to be content with the psychic results of such experiments and an asceticism departing from the true God. Fr Sophrony also warned against attributing too much significance to method, and he emphasized the importance of every invocation of the name of Christ being inseparably coupled with consciousness of the person of Christ. Results obtained by artificial means are not long-lasting and do not unite our spirit with the Spirit of the living God.[496] He described prayer as being like shafts of light cast into the dark depths of our inner life showing us the passions or attachments lodged therein. This should lead to increased feelings of repentance.[497] On the other hand, impersonal asceticism has led many towards self-divinization, seeing in the human being an absoluteness which is but a reflection of the divine absoluteness in the creature created in his likeness. He noted: "In these circumstances we open up for ourselves created beauty not the First Being. And in all of it there is no salvation for man."[498]

While the attitude of Orthodoxy may at first glance appear harsh towards non-Christian spirituality it highlights the importance of not losing sight of the uniqueness of the Christian Gospel and the divinity of Christ. Orthodox theology emphasizes the need for a personal encounter with Christ and receiving the gift of his divine energies for a person to realize divinization (*theosis*).[499]

Kallistos Ware has written: "No authentic relationship between persons can exist without mutual freedom and spontaneity, and this is true in particular of inner prayer."[500] Varying forms of prayer will therefore appeal to different people. While the Jesus Prayer is certainly not the only way of prayer, it is an ideal prayer for the reasons discussed in this book. It is particularly so for members of the Eastern Christian Churches in which this prayer tradition arose. Moreover, it is not associated with the problematic features that have attracted criticism of more innovative Meditation methods.

The Jesus Prayer is a verbal prayer which with God's grace may deepen into contemplative prayer. In the East, it has the advantage of coming to us enshrined in many centuries of continuous and hallowed tradition. Moreover, its practice has been elucidated by the testimony of innumerable saints and spiritual masters, including contemporary elders whose teachings continue to give guidance and protection from pitfalls. For many people the Jesus Prayer will undoubtedly remain a treasured path to direct union with the ever living and exalted Lord Jesus who bears "the name that is above every name" (Philippians 2:9).

Catholic perspectives

The Catholic Church has expressed many of the same concerns as the Orthodox authorities in relation to non-Christian influences and Christian prayer. These matters were outlined in detail by the Vatican Congregation for the Doctrine of the Faith in 1989. In its *Letter to the Bishops of the Catholic Church on Some Aspects of Christian Meditation* it was recognized that many of the faithful were asking what value non-Christian forms of Meditation might have for Christians.[501] Although noting that some people were turning to Eastern methods for therapeutic reasons, the document did not address itself to the psychological aspects, such as promoting inner peace or psychic balance. It focused instead on the spiritual and theological aspects. Given that many traditional methods of meditation had fallen into disuse, the question arose as to whether other hitherto foreign elements could be incorporated into the Christian tradition.[502]

It pointed out that Christian prayer "is always authentically personal and communitarian."[503] It requires a personal communion with the Persons of the Trinity and the avoidance of impersonal techniques or concentration on oneself which exclude openness to God. The document noted that grace must be sought from God as a gift and illumination does not render Christian faith superfluous. It also taught that the grace of the Holy Spirit cannot be equated with mere psychological experience and can even be achieved in affliction or desolation.[504]

It warns that attempts to fuse Christian meditation with that which is non-Christian is not free from dangers and errors. It noted that some people use such methods solely as psychophysical preparation for a truly Christian contemplation, but others have gone further and used techniques to try to generate spiritual experiences similar to those of certain Catholic mystics. Others have even sought to place the absolute, a property of Buddhist theory, on the same level as the majesty of God revealed in Christ. Using "negative theology" in this way risks abandoning the very idea of the One and Triune God "in favour of an immersion in the indeterminate abyss of divinity".[505] The document emphasized that it must be borne in mind that man is essentially a creature, and so absorbing the human self into the divine self is never possible. Christ's sharing of the divine nature with us does not suppress our created nature.[506] In Christian prayer the personal self and creaturehood are not dissolved and do not disappear into the absolute.[507]

The document acknowledged that what is true and holy in other religions is not to be rejected out of hand and "on the contrary, one can take from them what is useful so long as the Christian conception of prayer, its logic and requirements are never obscured."[508]

It also pointed out that the seeking of God through prayer has to be preceded and accompanied by ascetical struggle and purification from sin.[509] The document emphasized the dogmatic perspective that it is impossible to arrive at a perfect love of God if we ignore his giving of himself to us through his incarnate Son in whom, under the action of the Holy Spirit, we participate through grace in the interior life of God. Having quoted the text "Whoever has seen me has seen the Father" (John 14:9), it emphasized "the grasping of the divine reality in the human figure of Jesus, his eternal divine dimension in its temporal form." We can only be drawn into the life of God through Christ and not through our own efforts.[510]

Getting closer to God is not based on any technique in the strict sense of the word and is always a gift of God to one who knows himself to be unworthy.[511] The document recognized that "the position and demeanour of the body" has an influence on recollection and dispositions of the spirit.[512] It mentioned that the psychophysical symbolism valued in the Christian East is often absent in Western prayer and it noted that in the hesychastic tradition, posture, breathing and heart rhythm have had a role in the practice of the Jesus Prayer.[513] It also cautioned that physical sensations which can produce pleasant feelings such as quiet, relaxation, or phenomena of light and warmth are not to be equated with the authentic consolations of the Holy Spirit or one's moral state. It added:

> That does not mean that genuine practices of meditation which come from the Christian East and from the great non-Christian religions, which prove attractive to the man of today who is divided and disorientated, cannot constitute a suitable means of helping the person who prays to come before God with an interior peace, even in the midst of external pressures.[514]

The document advised that out of the varieties of Christian prayer, a person should seek and find his or her own forms of prayer, but in the end, they should "flow into the *way to the Father*". One should be led "not so much by personal tastes as by the Holy Spirit, who guides him, through Christ, to the Father."[515]

The letter noted that there are times of aridity in prayer when a person "feels" nothing of God. It cautions that this should not be immediately interpreted as the "dark night" in the mystical sense. Rather, such times test whether we have fidelity to seek God and go beyond our self-seeking and our "experiences".[516] The document concludes by stating that we can never place ourselves on the same level as God's love, the sole object of Christian contemplation. Proximity to the thrice-holy God produces humility and reverence.[517]

CHAPTER 13

The Jesus Prayer in Context

The name that is above every name ...
Philippians 2:9

Our exploratory journey to the Jesus Prayer draws to its conclusion. Having briefly reviewed in previous chapters some of the main traditions of Christian prayer in both the East and the West, we are now in a position to consider how they relate to each other and to the Jesus Prayer.

The historical perspective

Looking at the historical pathways we can see that the traditions of contemplative prayer in both East and West have ultimately derived from the early Christian centuries out of the traditions of the Desert Fathers. In the East the quest for unceasing prayer was expressed in the practice of "arrow prayers", which originally comprised repetitive brief phrases, mainly from the Psalms. Inspired by the Scriptures, particularly the New Testament tradition of veneration of the divine name, some prayers ultimately became expressed in the form of the words of the Jesus Prayer. Over the centuries this practice remained strong within Eastern Orthodoxy, particularly in the hesychastic tradition.

During the twentieth century, the Jesus Prayer became widely known beyond the boundaries of the Orthodox Church, and to some extent it became practised as a prayer detached from the liturgical and sacramental life of the Church. Moreover, the tradition of practising the prayer under the direction of a spiritual guide became less prominent due to the scarcity of people sufficiently experienced in the Jesus Prayer.

In monasteries in the West the practice of *lectio divina* became prominent with its four components of reading (*lectio*), meditation (*meditatio*), prayer (*oratio*), and contemplation (*contemplatio*). The portrayal by the Carthusian Guigo II in the twelfth century of *lectio divina* in terms of a ladder suggests that prayer was becoming viewed in terms of four sequential steps. In the era of Scholasticism these tended to be seen as different types of prayer appropriate for different types of people.

Another major prayer tradition in the Latin Church has been the Marian rosary, which for centuries has been an immensely widespread prayer practice. As discussed in chapter 4, the rosary differs from the Jesus Prayer in both its historical development and its content. It has a meditative element, in that themes centred on the life and saving actions of Christ are a focus of the prayer while the invocations to Mary are recited. It has a technical similarity to the Jesus Prayer because of the repeated invocations of a brief prayer formula and beads being utilized in a similar way to a prayer rope.

During the Protestant era the practice of contemplative prayer suffered setbacks from two competing forces. Many of the monasteries were suppressed by the Protestant Reformers, while the Catholic Inquisition was highly suspicious of any potentially heretical mystical movements. In the seventeenth century, the Catholic Church was concerned about the rise of Quietism, a mystical teaching that spiritual perfection was attained by passive contemplation of God, annihilation of the will and a passive withdrawal from actions in the world. Ultimately, contemplation became seen as a rare and exalted state suitable for spiritually advanced people such as monks and nuns in monasteries but not for lay people.[518] This view remained predominant in the Roman Catholic Church into modern times.

From our brief historical overview it can be seen that a *lectio divina* pattern in various forms served as the template for much of the contemplative prayer practice of the religious orders. The same basic components, albeit with certain variations, can be recognized in the Benedictine, Carthusian, Carmelite and Jesuit traditions. Although the *Spiritual Exercises* of Ignatius of Loyola involved a much more elaborate structure, they followed the same general sequence of meditative reflecting on a theme, imaginatively entering into the scene, then being led into a response of prayer. The Carmelite tradition also included the practice of the presence of God and prayers of aspiration similar to the "arrow prayers" of the Desert Fathers. Common to all these traditions was emphasis on prayer as a personal and loving encounter with Christ.

The apophatic tradition inspired by Pseudo-Dionysius and evident in *The Cloud of Unknowing* was also part of the spirituality of the West. The prayer practice described in *The Cloud*, in which discursive thought is bypassed and replaced with a reaching out in love to the incomprehensible God, appears at first glance to be very different to the *lectio divina* practice. This impression, however, is misleading, as we noted in chapter 6. The author gave due recognition to *lectio divina*, but he was addressing his teachings to persons well advanced in spiritual life, who were experiencing the powerful beginnings of God's mystical graces of contemplation. For them a simplified pattern of prayerful aspirations using a brief prayer-word imbued with fervour was more appropriate. This pattern is reminiscent of that "fiery outbreak" of prayer described by John Cassian. So, the spirituality evident in *The Cloud of Unknowing* is in fact mainstream. It is, in the words of William Johnston, "part of the great current of medieval spirituality".[519]

In the context of changes in the latter half of the twentieth century, the effects of a widespread lack of contemplative practices of prayer among Western Catholics began to have serious consequences. A spiritual hunger was apparent with many seeking a deeper inner life but feeling unsatisfied with the traditional Catholic prayer practices. Changes in society, the impact of the Second Vatican Council, greater acquaintance with Eastern non-Christian forms of Meditation, and greater knowledge of depth psychology, were all factors leading to many young people becoming dissatisfied with what they perceived as a lack of spiritual depth to their experiences in the Church. This led to an exodus and an exploration of other traditions.

Eastern Meditation traditions

Christian Meditation and the practice of Centering Prayer developed in the early 1970s and they have become popular practices since that time. They represented a response to the spread of practices from Eastern traditions and religions beginning to impact on the Catholic Church at that time. Yoga and Meditation techniques from Hinduism and Buddhism began to be utilized by many people in an effort to enhance their practice of Christian prayer. Such influences have not been without controversy. As discussed in chapter 12, the criticisms have hinged on whether these developments represent the introduction of incompatible alien traditions into Christian spirituality and whether they can constitute genuine Christian prayer.

In addressing these complex issues, the 1989 *Letter to the Bishops of the Catholic Church* emphasized the importance of maintaining the integrity of Christian prayer and avoiding its degradation by non-Christian elements. At the same time, it insisted that the Catholic Church does not reject what is true and holy in non-Christian religions. Accordingly, it stated that these ways of prayer should not be rejected out of hand simply because they are not Christian, but "one can take from them what is useful so long as the Christian conception of prayer, its logic and requirements are never obscured".[520]

The key issue to be determined is whether practices such as yoga and various forms of Eastern Meditation can be utilized in a way that can effectively prepare for, augment, or be part of Christian prayer. As we noted in chapter 5, the hesychastic tradition has probably been influenced by practices from Sufism and Hindu yoga, but these influences have been very peripheral and non-essential, and they have in no way compromised the integrity of prayer in this Christian tradition. In a similar way, notwithstanding the criticisms that have been raised, modern practices such as Christian Meditation or Centering Prayer may be acceptable options for people who find that they assist their capacity for recollection and practice of prayer. Nonetheless, it should be taken into account that one's prayer practice needs to have a personal, Christocentric focus to constitute Christian prayer. Moreover, one needs to be aware that there is no easy, simple, mechanistic procedure that can inexorably bring us into union with God.

Fr Sophrony Sakharov also warned against attempting to quickly or forcefully acquire spiritual gifts.[521] Furthermore, he is a very important witness from his own personal experience with both Buddhist Meditation and, later, with Christian prayer that there is "a radical difference between the Jesus Prayer and all other ascetic theories".[522] He recognized that it is possible through impersonal asceticism to experience phenomena such as mental stillness, a sense of awe, freedom of spirit and psychic beauty, but this had led many on a deluded path to self-contemplation and not the contemplation of God.[523]

Although the forms of Christian prayer in the East and the West have differed in their historical development, they have many common features. In this book, we have also noted the existence of a variety of practices containing elements which may be physical, psychological and/or spiritual, such as various schools of Meditation, yoga, and the psychophysical practices of the hesychasts. Although these practices do not constitute prayer per se, they may consist of ineffable experiences which accompany or lead into states of prayer or contemplation. They encompass a range of highly complex phenomena which are rich subject matter for scholars working at the interface of the disciplines of psychology, neurosciences, theology, spirituality, quantum physics and philosophy.

In-depth discussion of these practices, which involve altered states of consciousness, are well beyond the scope and purpose of this book. In some cases these techniques have been adapted for use as purely secular methods to improve physical or psychological health, such as the practice of Mindfulness Meditation as treatment for anxiety, depression and chronic pain syndromes. At the psychological and spiritual levels they may direct us towards our spiritual nature. They may evoke in us a sense of awe, wonder, joy and reverence, hopefully making us more attuned and receptive to the touch of God's grace. On the other hand, they confront us with potential dangers. Fr Sophrony has warned that non-Christian Meditation can confer such experiences and lead to self-glorification. He has written that what we can perceive in that state is "the natural genius of the human spirit in his sublimated impulses towards the

Absolute".[524] The created beauty manifested in this state is but a reflection of the beauty of God, who alone should be the object of our worship. True Christian prayer is a personal communication with God revealed to us in the person of Jesus.

Human effort and divine grace

Traditions such as Meditation which represent human attempts at spiritual development raise the question of the relationship between our natural human efforts and God's grace. Orthodox Christian tradition views this relationship as that of a synergy (*synergia*), notwithstanding the fact that the human effort alone is insufficient and in no way commensurate with God's action. In the Jesus Prayer the human actions of concentrative focus on the words of the prayer in harmony with the breathing rhythm no doubt convey some of the natural psychological and physical effects of Meditation practice, but the crucial invocation of the name and focus on the presence of Jesus conveys receptiveness to the action of divine grace. God's saving action involves "a mysterious *synergy* of human and divine wills interwoven without fusion".[525]

Jean-Yves Leloup, an Orthodox writer, provided an example of such synergy in his account of a monk on Mount Athos, whom he called "Fr Seraphim", responding to a young man who questioned him about prayer. The first response of the monk was to direct the young man to focus on themes in nature. Following the advice to "meditate like a mountain" gave the young man stability, good posture and a sense of eternity. When told to "meditate like a poppy", his orientation of turning toward the light and bending with the wind evoked a sense of humility. Meditating "like the ocean", the ebb and flow of his breath like the waves, taught him that thoughts come and go like waves, while the depths below remain still. When told to meditate "like a bird", sounds like that of the cooing of nearby turtledoves rising up from within led him to repeat "*Kyrie eleison, Kyrie eleison* . . . " The invocation gradually entered his heart, leading into silence.

There was a transition from the purely natural level when Fr Seraphim instructed the young man to meditate "like Abraham". This entering into the realm of faith personalized the Absolute, naming it as God and Creator. Leloup described this change: "The difference between Nature and God is the difference between the blue of the sky and the blue of one's eyes. Abraham was in search of those eyes." This change required practising hospitality like Abraham, trust and abandonment of self in sacrifice. Finally, the old monk told him that one day the cry of "Abba" would arise not from his lips but from the depths of his heart. After a few more months "the Jesus Prayer swept him into the abyss" such that he felt able to say with Paul that it was no longer he who lived but Christ living in him (Galatians 2:20). Soon after, the young man was told to leave Mount Athos and return home.[526]

A precious gem

In the light of the issues discussed in previous chapters of this book it is apparent that the Jesus Prayer from the East shares the valuable features of the Christian prayer traditions of the West. Commencing as a verbal prayer pleading for God's mercy and light, it can progress over time into more interior prayer leading into silence (*hesychia*) just as discursive meditation can lead to contemplation in the *lectio divina* tradition. There is the same sequence from active human effort ultimately yielding to the action of God in infused contemplation. The Jesus Prayer includes the benefits of Meditation while being an ideal Christian prayer.

Although unceasing prayer in the literal sense of constant repetitions is not a practical possibility in the midst of many of our daily activities, the frequent practice of the Jesus Prayer nurtures an abiding and loving awareness of the divine presence. Although it is not a mantra, there are clearly some mantra-like characteristics in the sense that there is a repetitive focus upon a formula of words, which narrows the thought processes and facilitates their moving deeper to the level of the heart. There is a reaching out into the ineffable depths of the spirit. Its methodology is simple and flexible, and it is not to be practised in a rigid or mechanical way. Consistent with the teachings of Teresa of Avila, progress depends upon cultivating virtues, particularly humility, love, detachment, repentance and perseverance. The prayer is said while focusing on the presence of Jesus and the meaning of the words being articulated. In accord with two of the methods of prayer enumerated by Ignatius of Loyola, the Jesus Prayer involves focus on the actual words of the prayer, and it is also often practised in synchrony with the breathing rhythm.

It also conforms to the recommendation of John Climacus to invoke the name of Jesus (Step 21), remember Jesus with every breath (Step 27), and "enclose your mind within the words of your prayer" (Step 28).[527] Any use of mental imagery during the Jesus Prayer is a practice strictly discouraged by the Eastern teachers.

Mere reliance on a method or technique is insufficient. Michael Casey OCSO has pointed out that no particular practice guarantees that we can infallibly reach our goal. In his words: "God will not be organized."[528] In discussing how prayer is integrated into our lives he has noted that the Western Fathers insist "that prayer comes as part of a package. It is imbedded in a network of supportive practices: interior and exterior, individual and communal, spontaneous and routine."[529]

Similarly, in the East, a major benefit of the Jesus Prayer is that it is embedded in an existing and ancient Christian tradition with a well-developed psychological, theological and spiritual framework. It is not a magic formula isolated from the life of the Church and it is integrated with the liturgical services, participation in the Christian mysteries (sacraments) and following the commandments of Christ. These elements are mutually reinforcing and nourish each other. For this reason, the tendency to divorce the Jesus Prayer from its broader context within the Church is undesirable and compromises its capacity to promote our spiritual growth. It is not merely a technique but part of a way of life.

The crowning jewel, as it were, of the Jesus Prayer is the holy name of Jesus, investing the prayer with power and divine energy, and leading us into his presence. As previously described, invoking the name of Jesus with faith has a sacramental quality. It is like a verbal icon putting us into direct contact with Jesus himself, seeking his mercy and grace. Moreover, with God's grace it may eventually blossom into "non-iconic" contemplative prayer. Its explicit focus on the name which is above all names makes it a form of prayer that can be readily embraced by all Christians.

Although we have reached the goal of discovering the Jesus Prayer, if you wish to practice this prayer, you now approach a new horizon. It must be acknowledged, of course, that because prayer is such a personal and individual matter involving our intimate relationship with God, there are many forms of valid and fruitful prayer. In a sense there are as many forms of prayer as there are individual persons. Yet, notwithstanding the fact that other forms of prayer can be equally beneficial, I trust that this book has demonstrated that the Jesus Prayer is a great spiritual treasure. I am therefore confident that readers who belong to an Eastern Church, whether Catholic or Orthodox, as well as readers from other Christian denominations, will realize that they have no need to look beyond the Jesus Prayer to greatly enrich their spiritual lives.

With the Jesus Prayer we can follow the example of the tax collector in the Gospel parable and cry out in repentance for God's mercy to heal and forgive our brokenness. Emulating the blind beggar near Jericho, we can raise our voices to Jesus with determination, faith and perseverance, begging for his uncreated energies to give us light, illumination and transformation. With the sweet nourishment of the repeated invocations of the name of Jesus we can direct our yearnings with hope that "all of us, with unveiled faces, seeing the glory of the Lord as though reflected in a mirror, are being transformed into the same image from one degree of glory to another" (2 Corinthians 3:18). Furthermore, we can be encouraged by the teaching of St Seraphim of Sarov that:

> In order to receive and to feel in one's heart the light of Christ, one should draw away one's attention as much as possible from all visible objects. Then, first having purified the soul by repentance and good deeds, and with a sincere faith in the Crucified, one should close one's bodily eyes, immerse the mind in the heart and cry and call incessantly the name of our Lord Jesus Christ. Then, in proportion to the zeal and ardour of spirit towards the Beloved, man finds in the Name that he is invoking a delight which will prompt him to search for the highest illumination.[530]

While practising the prayer involves effort and spiritual struggle, it also brings us to Jesus and his festival of joy. In other words, we experience the Cross as well as the life of the Resurrection, which we can begin to live even during our earthly life. Beyond that, the following words of Fr Sophrony Sakharov are applicable, and they make a fitting conclusion to the theme of this book:

> To acquire prayer is to acquire eternity. When the body lies dying, the cry "Jesus Christ" becomes the garment of the soul; when the brain no longer functions and other prayers are difficult to remember, in the light of the divine knowledge that proceeds from the name our spirit will rise into life incorruptible.[531]

This is the Christian hope.

"Amen. Come, Lord Jesus!" (Revelation 22:20)

Appendix

Suggestions for the Practice of the Jesus Prayer

As we have previously noted, the Jesus Prayer can be said informally at any time when doing routine daily activities, and it can also be practised in a fixed form in which regular time periods are set aside to be devoted specifically to the prayer.

In the tradition of the Orthodox East, an experienced elder would give personal instructions to the spiritual aspirant about how to practise the Jesus Prayer. Specific details such as the timing and duration of the prayer sessions and other practical matters would be individually determined by the elder who would manifest his wisdom and insight to meet the individual characteristics, needs and circumstances of the spiritual seeker.

Given the potential hazards of the spiritual path, we should always seek to find an experienced spiritual guide for our practice of the Jesus Prayer. Such a person is important in providing support, encouragement, insight and help on the spiritual path and in managing difficulties that arise in our prayer practice.

It remains advisable that many of the specific details for formally practising the Jesus Prayer at set times should be determined only under the ongoing guidance of a suitably trained spiritual director or teacher experienced in praying the Jesus Prayer. For similar reasons, a person in emotional distress or with a history of psychological or psychiatric disturbance should seek advice and supervision from medical or mental health professionals before practising regular formal prayer sessions. Such guidance and support becomes particularly necessary if any unusual mental states or distress begin to be experienced in deeper meditative states of prayer. It should also be sought if prolonged prayer sessions of greater than twenty to thirty minutes duration or frequency of more than twice daily are being considered.

Despite these precautionary observations, there are some generally accepted practical measures which can be recommended in the practice of the Jesus Prayer:

Whenever possible, the prayer should be said in a quiet, peaceful place and in a suitable setting, such as before an icon.

- The preferred times for prayer are either the early morning before the distractions of the day have commenced or, alternatively, at night-time.
- Saying a few introductory verbal prayers such as the Lord's Prayer is a good way to "warm up" prior to commencing the Jesus Prayer itself.
- The essential feature is to focus on the presence of Jesus with love and devotion, addressing him by name.
- To begin with, the words of the prayer should be audible to oneself, even if they are softly spoken or whispered. Hearing the sound of the words assists with concentration.
- The wording can comprise the full version: "Lord Jesus Christ, Son of God, have mercy on me, a sinner" or any of the variations. The exact wording can be varied according to one's preference or feeling but the essential requirement is that the words contain the holy name of Jesus.
- Addressing Jesus who is present before you, start to slowly say the words of the prayer. Aim to keep repeating the words slowly and calmly for the duration of the period of prayer.
- Try to keep your whole mind within the words of the prayer.
- Keeping the eyes closed is advisable to minimize distractions.
- Do not try to visualize Jesus or anything else.
- While there is flexibility in relation to posture during the prayer, generally a seated upright posture is advisable, because it is more conducive to alertness and concentration.
- Periodically changing posture, especially bowing in veneration (*metanias*), making the sign of the cross, or making prostrations may be helpful.

- Staying alert is important. So, if you feel drowsy, it is best to stand up for a short time, making a sign of the cross or performing some prostrations to help reduce sleepiness.
- With practice the prayer tends to move from being an audible verbal prayer to being said mentally. Nonetheless we should not hesitate to move back to saying the prayer aloud as required, particularly if our concentration has wandered.
- The use of a prayer rope or chaplet (*komvoschoinion* or *tchotki*) can assist with concentration as you say the words of the prayer once for each knot held between thumb and finger.
- If you are drawn into wordless silence let your attention remain focused on Jesus. Whenever you become self-conscious of being in a silent state or aware of your thoughts wandering elsewhere, stay calm and gently return your focus again to addressing the prayer to Jesus.
- You may notice, as you say the prayer, that it falls naturally into synchrony with your breathing rhythm.
- Breathing should not be intentionally forced. You may let the words "Lord, Jesus Christ, Son of God" naturally begin to coincide with your inward breath and the other words coincide with the outward breath. This is often helpful, but it is potentially dangerous to try to consciously manipulate the breathing rhythm according to more complex patterns or ratios such as occur in the practice of yoga. Similarly, there should be no effort to change or interfere with your heartbeat.

Under no circumstances should we try to force our progress in the prayer.

While the Jesus Prayer is usually practised alone as a private prayer, it can occur in a group setting. In a group, different members can, in turn, say the prayer a set number of times.

Suggested Further Reading

Anonymous, *The Way of the Pilgrim: and The Pilgrim Continues His Way*, tr. R. M. French (New York: Harper Collins Publishers, 1991).

Barrington-Ward, Simon, *The Jesus Prayer: A Way to Contemplation* (Boston, MA: Pauline Books, 2011).

Brianchaninov, Ignatius, *On the Prayer of Jesus*, tr. Fr Lazarus (Boston, MA: New Seeds Books, 2006).

Deseille, Archimandrite Placide, "The Hesychast Prayer in the Orthodox Church", in Coomaraswamy, Rama, *The Invocation of the Name of Jesus: As Practiced in the Western Church* (Louisville, KY: Fons Vitae, 1999).

Gillet, Lev (A Monk of the Eastern Church), *On the Invocation of the Name of Jesus* (Springfield, IL: Templegate Publishers, 1985).

Golynsky-Mihailovsky, Archbishop Anthony, *Two Elders on the Jesus Prayer*, comp. and ed. N. M. Novikov, tr. Igor V. Ksenzov (Hayesville, OH: Skete of the Entrance of the Theotokos into the Temple, 2008).

Hester, David, *The Jesus Prayer: A Gift from the Fathers* (Ben Lomond, CA: Conciliar Press, 2001).

Maloney, George, SJ, *Prayer of the Heart* (Notre Dame, IN: Ave Maria Press, 1981).

Mathewes-Green, Frederica, *The Jesus Prayer: The Ancient Desert Prayer that Tunes the Heart to God* (Brewster, MA: Paraclete Press, 2009).

Sakharov, Sophrony, *On Prayer*, tr. Rosemary Edmonds (Crestwood, NY: St Vladimir's Seminary Press, 1996).

Ware, Kallistos, *The Power of the Name* (Fairacres, Oxford: SLG Press, 1986).

Ware, Kallistos, *The Jesus Prayer* (London: Catholic Truth Society, 2014).

Zaleski, Irma, *Living the Jesus Prayer* (New York: Continuum, 1997).

Bibliography

The Ascetic Homilies of Saint Isaac the Syrian, Homily 65 (Boston, MA: Holy Transfiguration Monastery, 2011).
The Carmelite Directory of the Spiritual Life (Chicago, IL: The Carmelite Press, 1951).
The Rule of St. Basil in Latin and English, tr. Anna M. Silvas (Collegeville, MN: Liturgical Press, 2013).
The Wisdom of Saint Isaac the Syrian, tr. Sebastian Brock (Fairacres, Oxford: SLG Press, 1997).
Abba Philimon, "A Discourse on Abba Philimon", in *The Philokalia*, Vol. 2, tr. and ed. G. E. H. Palmer, Philip Sherrard and Kallistos Ware (London and Boston: Faber and Faber, 1981), pp. 343–57.
American Psychiatric Association, *Diagnostic and Statistical Manual of Mental Disorders (DSM-5)* (5th edn, Arlington, VA: American Psychiatric Publishing, 2013).
A Monk of Mount Athos, *The Watchful Mind: Teachings on the Prayer of the Heart*, tr. George Dokos (Yonkers, NY: St Vladimir's Seminary Press, 2014).
Anonymous, *The Cloud of Unknowing and the Book of Privy Counselling*, tr. and ed. William Johnston (New York: Image Books, 2014).
Anonymous, *The Way of the Pilgrim: and The Pilgrim Continues His Way*, tr. R. M. French (New York: Harper Collins Publishers, 1991).
A Priest of the Byzantine Church, *Reflections on the Jesus Prayer* (Denville, NJ: Dimension Books, 1978).
Arraj, James, *From St John of the Cross to Us: The Story of a 400 Year Long Misunderstanding and What it Means for the Future of Christian Mysticism* (Chiloquin, OR: Inner Growth Books, 1999).

Arraj, James and St. Romain, Philip (eds), *Critical Questions in Christian Contemplative Practice* (Midland, OR: Inner Growth Books, 2007).
Athanasius the Great, *Against the Heathen*, Vol. 25 in Migne, Jacques-Paul (ed.), *Patrologia Graeca (PG) Cursus Completus* (Paris, 1863), p. 65.
Athanasius the Great, *On the Incarnation*, Vol. 25 in Migne, Jacques-Paul (ed.), *Patrologia Graeca (PG) Cursus Completus* (Paris, 1863), pp. 125, 192.
Augustine, "Discourse on Psalm 37", in *Enarrationes in Psalmos: Vol. II. Psalms 30–37*, tr. Scholastica Hebgin and Felicitas Corrigan (London: Green & Co., 1961), p. 344.
Augustine, "Letter to Proba", in *Letters of St Augustine of Hippo*, tr. J. G. Cunningham (Edinburgh: T&T Clark, 1875), pp. 155–6.
Baker, Augustine, *Holy Wisdom Or Directions For The Prayer of Contemplation* (London: Burns and Oates, 1911).
Barrington-Ward, Simon, *The Jesus Prayer: A Way to Contemplation* (Boston, MA: Pauline Books, 2011).
Barrington-Ward, Simon and Brother Ramon, *Praying the Jesus Prayer Together* (Peabody, MA: Hendrickson Publishers, 2004).
Basham, Arthur L., *The Wonder that was India* (New Delhi: Rupa & Co., 1994).
Bloom, Metropolitan Anthony, *Asceticism (Somatopsychic Techniques in Greek Orthodox Christianity*, Guild Lecture No. 95 (London: The Guild of Pastoral Psychology, October 1957).
Bourgeault, Cynthia, *Centering Prayer and Inner Awakening* (Lanham, MD: Cowley Publications, 2004).
Brianchaninov, Ignatius, *On the Prayer of Jesus*, tr. Fr Lazarus (Boston, MA: New Seeds Books, 2006).
Brother Lawrence of the Resurrection, *Writings and Conversations On The Practice of the Presence of God*, tr. Salvatore Sciurba OCD (Washington, DC: Institute of Carmelite Studies, 1994).
Bungė, Gabriel, *Earthen Vessels: The Practice of Personal Prayer According to the Patristic Tradition*, tr. Michael J. Miller (San Francisco: Ignatius Press, 2002).

Campbell, Antony F., *The Study Companion to Old Testament Literature: An Approach to the Writings of Pre-Exilic and Exilic Israel*, Old Testament Studies 2 (Wilmington, DL: Michael Glazier, 1989).

Casey, Michael, OCSO, *Strangers to the City: Reflections on the Beliefs and Values of the Rule of Saint Benedict* (Brewster, MA: Paraclete Press, 2013).

Chrysostomos, *A Guide to Orthodox Psychotherapy: The Science, Theology, and Spiritual Practice Behind It and Its Clinical Application* (Lanham, MD: University Press of America, 2007).

Coloe, Mary, *God Dwells with Us: Temple Symbolism in the Fourth Gospel* (Collegeville, MN: Liturgical Press, 2001).

Congregation for the Doctrine of the Faith, *Letter to the Bishops of the Catholic Church on some aspects of Christian meditation* (15 October, 1989), <http://www.vatican.va/roman_curia/congregations/cfaith/documents/rc_con_cfaith_doc_19891015_meditazione-cristiana_en.html>, accessed 28 May 2019.

Coomaraswamy, Rama, *The Invocation of the Name of Jesus: As Practiced in the Western Church* (Louisville, KY: Fons Vitae, 1999).

Coward, Harold and Goa, David, *Mantra: Hearing the Divine in India* (Chambersburg, PA: Anima Books, 1991).

Culligan, Kevin, "The Dark Night and Depression", in Egan, Keith J. (ed.), *Carmelite Prayer: A Tradition for the 21st Century* (Mahwah, NJ: Paulist Press, 2003), pp. 130–5.

Cuttat, Jacques-Albert, *The Encounter of Religions: A Dialogue between the West and the Orient with an Essay on the Prayer of Jesus*, tr. Pierre de Fontnouvelle with Evis McGrew (New York: Desclée Company, 1960).

Danker, Frederick William (ed.), *A Greek-English Lexicon of the New Testament and other Early Christian Literature*, 3rd edn (Chicago and London: University of Chicago Press, 2000).

Déchanet, J.-M., *Christian Yoga*, tr. Roland Hindmarsh (London: Burns and Oates, 1964).

Delmonte, Michael, "Mantras and Meditation", *Perceptual and Motor Skills* 57 (1983), pp. 64–6.

De Mello, Anthony, *Sadhana: A Way to God—Christian Exercises in Eastern Form* (New York: Image Books, Doubleday, 1984).

Deseille, Archimandrite Placide, "The Hesychast Prayer in the Orthodox Church", in Coomaraswamy, Rama, *The Invocation of the Name of Jesus: As Practiced in the Western Church* (Louisville, KY: Fons Vitae, 1999), pp. 217–54.

Diadochos of Photiki, "On Spiritual Knowledge and Discrimination: One Hundred Texts-85", *The Philokalia*, Vol. 1, tr. and ed. G. E. H. Palmer, Philip Sherrard and Kallistos Ware (London: Faber and Faber Ltd, 1983), p. 285.

Dulles, Avery, SJ, in *The Spiritual Exercises of St Ignatius*, tr. Louis J. Puhl, SJ (New York: Vintage Books, 2000), pp. xix–xx.

Dupuche, John R., "Sufism and Hesychasm", in Bronwen Neil, Geoffrey D. Dunn and Lawrence Cross (eds), *Prayer and Spirituality in the Early Church: Liturgy and Life* III (Strathfield, NSW: St Paul's Publications, 2003), pp. 335–44.

Egan, Keith J. (ed.), *Carmelite Prayer: A Tradition for the 21st Century* (Mahwah, NJ: Paulist Press, 2003).

Eliade, Mircea, *Yoga: Immortality and Freedom* (Princeton, NJ: Princeton University Press, 1969).

Ellenberger, Henri, *The Discovery of the Unconscious: The History and Evolution of Dynamic Psychiatry* (New York: Basic Books, 1970).

Evagrios the Solitary, "On Prayer: One Hundred and Fifty-Three Texts-71", *The Philokalia*, Vol. 1, tr. and ed. G. E. H. Palmer, Philip Sherrard and Kallistos Ware (London: Faber and Faber Ltd, 1983), p. 63.

Evagrius of Pontus, *The Greek Ascetic Corpus*, tr. and ed. Robert E. Sinkewicz (Oxford: Oxford University Press, 2003).

Evagrius Ponticus, *The Praktikos and Chapters on Prayer*, tr. John Eudes Bamberger (Collegeville, MN: Cistercian Publications/ Liturgical Press, 1972).

Farasiotis, Dionysios, *The Gurus, the Young Man, and Elder Paisios* (Platina, CA: Saint Herman of Alaska Brotherhood, 2008).

Forest, Jim, *Praying with Icons* (Maryknoll, NY: Orbis, 1997).

Franck, Adolphe, *The Kabbalah: The Religious Philosophy of the Hebrews* (Secaucus, NJ: The Citadel Press, 1967).

Fry, Timothy, OSB (ed.), *The Rule of St. Benedict in English* (Collegeville, MN: Liturgical Press, 1982).
Gallagher, Timothy, *The Discernment of Spirits: An Ignatian Guide for Everyday Living* (New York: Crossroad, 2005).
Gillet, Lev (A Monk of the Eastern Church), *On the Invocation of the Name of Jesus* (Springfield, IL: Templegate Publishing, 1985).
Gillet, Lev (A Monk of the Eastern Church), *The Jesus Prayer* (Crestwood, NY: St Vladimir's Seminary Press, 1987).
Goleman, Daniel and Davidson, Richard J., *The Science of Meditation: How to Change Your Brain, Mind and Body* (London: Penguin Life, 2017).
Golynsky-Mihailovsky, Archbishop Anthony, *Two Elders on the Jesus Prayer*, ed. and comp. N. M. Novikov and tr. V. Ksenzov (Hayesville, OH: Skete of the Entrance of the Theotokos into the Temple, 2008).
Gonda, Jan, "The Indian Mantra", *Oriens* 16 (1963), p. 246.
Gregory of Nyssa, *On the Soul and the Resurrection*, tr. Catharine P. Roth (Crestwood, NY: St Vladimir's Seminary Press, 1993).
Gregory Palamas, "Homily Thirty One", in *The Homilies*, tr. and ed. Christopher Vemiamin (Waymart, PA: Mount Thabor Publishing, 2009), pp. 243–50.
Gregory Palamas, *The Triads*, tr. Nicholas Gendle (Mahwah, NJ: Paulist Press, 1983), p. 51.
Grof, Christina and Grof, Stanislav, *The Stormy Search for the Self: A Guide to Personal Growth through Transformational Crisis* (New York: Tarcher/Putnam Books, 1990).
Gross, Rita N., "Meditation and Prayer", *Buddhist–Christian Studies* 22 (2002), pp. 77–86.
Guillamont, Antoine, "The Jesus Prayer among the Monks of Egypt", *Eastern Churches Review* 6, pp. 66–71.
Gwynn, Mark and Laugesen, Amanda (eds), *Australian Concise Oxford Dictionary of Current English*, 6th edn (Melbourne: Oxford University Press, 2017).
Habra, Fr George, "The Sources of the Doctrine of Gregory Palamas on the Divine Energies", *Eastern Churches Quarterly* 12:6 (1957–8), p. 245.

Harris, Paul, *John Main: A Biography in Text and Photos* (Catalina, AZ: Medio Media Publishing, 2001).

Hausherr, Irénée, *The Name of Jesus* (Collegeville, MN: Cistercian Publications/Liturgical Press, 2008).

Hester, David, *The Jesus Prayer: A Gift from the Fathers* (Ben Lomond, CA: Conciliar Press, 2001).

Hesychios the Priest, "On Watchfulness and Holiness (196)", *The Philokalia*, Vol. 1, tr. and ed. G. E. H. Palmer, Philip Sherrard and Kallistos Ware (London: Faber and Faber, 1983), p. 197.

House, Mark A. (ed.), *Compact Greek-English Lexicon of the New Testament* (Peabody, MA: Hendrickson Publishers, 2008).

Ignatius of Loyola, *Personal Writings: Reminiscences, Spiritual Diary, Select Letters including the text of The Spiritual Exercises*, tr. Joseph A. Munitiz and Philip Endean (London: Penguin Books, 1996).

Ignatius of Loyola, *The Spiritual Exercises*, tr. Michael Ivens, SJ (Leominster, Herefordshire: Gracewing, 2004).

Irenaeus, *Against Heresies*, tr. John Keble (Oxford: James Parker and Co., 1872).

Ivens, Michael, SJ, *Understanding the Spiritual Exercises: Text and Commentary—A Handbook for Retreat Directors* (Leominster: Gracewing, 1998).

John Cassian, *Conferences*, tr. Colm Luibheid (Mahwah, NJ: Paulist Press, 1985).

John Climacus, *The Ladder of Divine Ascent*, tr. Colm Luibheid and Norman Russell (Mahwah, NJ: Paulist Press, 1982).

John of the Cross, *Dark Night of the Soul*, tr. Mirabai Starr (New York: Riverhead Books, 2003).

John of the Cross, "The Ascent of Mount Carmel" in *The Collected Works of St John of the Cross,* tr. Kieran Kavanaugh and Otilio Rodriguez (Washington, DC: ICS Publications, 1973), p. 289.

John of the Cross, "The Dark Night", in *The Collected Works of St John of the Cross*, tr. Kieran Kavanaugh and Otilio Rodriguez (Washington, DC: ICS Publications, 1973), pp. 293-389.

John of Damascus, *On the Orthodox Faith*, Vol. 94 in Migne, Jacques-Paul (ed.), *Patrologia Graeca (PG) Cursus Completus* (Paris, 1863), pp. 798, 924 and 928.

Johnston, William, SJ, *Mystical Theology: The Science of Love* (London: Harper Collins, 1995).
Johnston, William, SJ, *Mystical Journey: An Autobiography* (Maryknoll, NY: Orbis, 2006).
Johnston, William, SJ (tr. and ed.), *The Cloud of Unknowing* and *The Book of Privy Counselling* (New York: Image Books, 2014).
Kavanaugh, Kieran, OCD, "Contemplation and the Stream of Consciousness", in Egan, Keith J. (ed.), *Carmelite Prayer: A Tradition for the 21st Century* (Mahwah, NJ: Paulist Press, 2003), pp. 102–4.
Keating, Thomas, OSCO, *The Mystery of Christ: The Liturgy as Spiritual Experience* (New York: Continuum, 1987).
Keating, Thomas, OCSO, *Open Mind, Open Heart: The Contemplative Dimension of the Gospel, 20th Anniversary Edition* (New York: Continuum, 2006).
Keating, Thomas, OCSO, *Invitation to Love: The Way of Christian Contemplation* (London: Bloomsbury, 2011).
Kenneth, Klaus, *Born to Hate—Reborn to Love: A Spiritual Odyssey from Head to Heart* (Dalton, PA: Mount Thabor Publishing, 2012).
King, Ursula, "A Response to Reflections on Buddhist and Christian Religious Practices", *Buddhist–Christian Studies* 22 (2002), pp. 105–12.
Kuijpers, H. J. H., van der Heijden, F. M. M. A., Tuinier, S. and Verhoeven, W. M. A., "Meditation induced Psychosis", *Psychopathology* 40 (2007), pp. 461–4.
Larchet, Jean-Claude, *Mental Disorders and Spiritual Healing: Teachings from the Early Christian East*, tr. Rama P. Coomaraswamy and G. John Champoux (Hillsdale, NY: Sophia Perennis, 2005).
Larkin, Ernest, "The Carmelite Tradition and Centering Prayer/Christian Meditation", in Egan, Keith J. (ed.), *Carmelite Prayer: A Tradition for the 21st Century* (Mahwah, NJ: Paulist Press, 2003), pp. 38–60.
Lazarus, Arthur A., "Psychiatric Problems Precipitated by Transcendental Meditation", *Psychological Reports* 39 (1976), pp. 601–2.

Leloup, Fr Jean-Yves, *Being Still: Reflections on an Ancient Mystical Tradition*, tr. M. S. Baird (Mahwah, NJ: Paulist Press, 2003).

Lossky, Vladimir, *The Mystical Theology of the Eastern Church* (Crestwood, NY: St Vladimir's Seminary Press, 1976).

MacCulloch, Diarmaid, *Silence: A Christian History* (London: Penguin Books, 2014).

McGee, Michael, "Meditation and Psychiatry", *Psychiatry* 5:1 (2008), pp. 28–41.

McKenzie, John L., *Dictionary of the Bible* (London: Geoffrey Chapman, 1965).

Main, John, *The Inner Christ* (London: Darton, Longman and Todd, 1987).

Main, John, *Christian Meditation: The Gethsemani Talks* (Tucson, AZ: Medio Media Publishing, 2001).

Main, John, *Word Into Silence*, ed. Laurence Freeman (Norwich: Canterbury Press, 2006).

Maloney, George A., *Prayer of the Heart* (Notre Dame, IN: Ave Maria Press, 1981).

Markides, Kyriacos C., *Inner River: A Pilgrimage to the Heart of Christian Spirituality* (New York: Image Books, 2012).

Mathewes-Green, Frederica, *The Jesus Prayer: The Ancient Desert Prayer that Tunes the Heart to God* (Brewster, MA: Paraclete Press, 2009).

Matus, Thomas, *Yoga and the Jesus Prayer Tradition: An Experiment in Faith* (Ramsey, NJ: Paulist Press, 1984).

May, Gerald G., *The Dark Night of the Soul: A Psychiatrist Explores the Connection between Darkness and Spiritual Growth* (New York: Harper San Francisco, 2005).

Maximus the Confessor, "Third Century on Love", in *The Philokalia*, Vol. 2, tr. and ed. G. E. H. Palmer, Philip Sherrard and Kallistos Ware (London: Faber and Faber, 1990), p. 88.

Meissner, William, SJ, *Ignatius of Loyola: The Psychology of a Saint* (New York: Yale University Press, 1992).

Melling, David J., "Hesychasm", in Parry, Ken et al (eds), *The Blackwell Dictionary of Eastern Christianity* (Oxford: Blackwell Publishers, 1999, pp. 230–1.

Meninger, William A., OCSO, *The Loving Search for God: Contemplative Prayer in the Cloud of Unknowing* (New York: Continuum, 2012).
Merton, Thomas, *Contemplative Prayer* (London: Darton, Longman and Todd, 1973).
Metzger, Bruce M. and Coogan, Michael D. (eds), *The Oxford Companion to the Bible* (Oxford: Oxford University Press, 1993).
Meyendorff, John, *St. Gregory Palamas and Orthodox Spirituality* (Crestwood, NY: St Vladimir's Seminary Press, 1974).
Meyendorff, John, *Christ in Eastern Christian Thought* (Crestwood, NY: St Vladimir's Seminary Press, 1975).
Migne, Jacques-Paul (ed.), *Patrologia Graeca (PG) Cursus Completus*, (Paris, 1863).
Migne, Jacques-Paul (ed.), *Patrologia Latina (PL) Cursus Completus*, (Paris, 1874).
Mother Maria of Normanby, *The Jesus Prayer: The Meeting of East and West in the Prayer of the Heart* (Newport Pagnell: Lovat Press, 1972).
Nikiphoros the Monk, "On Watchfulness and the Guarding of the Heart", in *The Philokalia*, Vol. 4, tr. and ed. G. E. H. Palmer, Philip Sherrard and Kallistos Ware (London: Faber and Faber Ltd, 1998), pp. 205–6.
Oberhammer, Gerhard, "The Use of Mantra in Yogic Meditation: The Testimony of the Pāśupata", in Alper, Harvey P. (ed.), *Understanding Mantras* (Albany, NY: State University of New York Press, 1989), p. 204.
O'Keefe, Mark, OSB, *The Way of Transformation: St Teresa of Avila on the Foundation and Fruit of Prayer* (Washington, DC: ICS Publications, 2016).
The Orthodox Study Bible (Nashville, TN: Thomas Nelson Inc., 2008).
Padoux, André, "Mantras—What Are They?", in Alper, Harvey P. (ed.), *Understanding Mantras* (Albany, NY: State University of New York Press, 1989), pp. 295–318.
Peeters, Tim, *When Silence Speaks: The Spiritual Way of the Carthusian Order* (London: Darton, Longman and Todd, 2015).

Pennington, M. Basil, OCSO, *Centering Prayer: Renewing an Ancient Christian Prayer Form* (New York: Image, Doubleday, 2001).

The Philokalia, Volumes 1–4, tr. and ed. G. E. H. Palmer, Philip Sherrard and Kallistos Ware (London and Boston: Faber and Faber, 1979–95).

Poslusney, Venard, *Prayer, Aspiration and Contemplation* (New York: Alba House, 1975).

Pseudo-Macarius, *The Fifty Spiritual Homilies and The Great Letter*, tr. and ed. George A. Maloney (Mahwah, NJ: Paulist Press, 1992).

Puretzki, N. and the Monastery of Sarov, *The Life and Teaching of Saint Seraphim of Sarov* (The Hague: Gozalov Books, 2008).

Ramsey, Boniface, OP, *Beginning to Read the Fathers*, (rev. edn, Mahwah, NJ: Paulist Press, 2012).

Raya, Joseph, *The Face of God* (Denville, NJ: Dimension Books, 1976).

Romain, Philip, *The Kundalini Process: A Christian Perspective* (Bel Aire, KS: Lulu Press, 2017).

Romanides, John S., *Patristic Theology: The University Lectures of Fr John Romanides* (Thessaloniki, Greece: Uncut Mountain Press, 2008).

Rose, Seraphim, *Orthodoxy and the Religion of the Future* (Platina, CA: Saint Herman of Alaska Brotherhood, 2004).

Rossini, Connie, *Is Centering Prayer Catholic? Fr Thomas Keating Meets Teresa of Avila and the CDF* (New Ulm, MN: Four Waters Press, 2015).

Ryan, Thomas, *Prayer of Heart and Body: Meditation and Yoga as Christian Spiritual Practice* (Mahwah, NJ: Paulist Press, 1995).

Sakharov, Sophrony, *His Life is Mine*, tr. Rosemary Edmonds (Crestwood, NY: St. Vladimir's Seminary Press, 1977).

Sakharov, Sophrony, *On Prayer*, tr. Rosemary Edmonds (Crestwood, NY: St. Vladimir's Seminary Press, 1998).

Sculley, Max, DLS, "Christian Meditation: Pseudo-Contemplation", <http://www.christendom-awake.org/pages/book-promotions/yoga-tai-chi&reiki/cmpseudo.htm>, (accessed 11 Mar. 2018).

Shapiro, Shauna L., Walsh, Roger and Britton, Willoughby B., "An Analysis of Recent Meditation Research and Suggestions for Future Directions", *Journal for Meditation and Meditation Research*, 3 (2003), pp. 69–90.

Sjögren, Per-Olaf, *The Jesus Prayer*, tr. Sydney Linton (London: SPCK, 1975).

Stewart, Columba, OSB, *Cassian the Monk* (New York: Oxford University Press, 1998).

Symeon the New Theologian, "Other Theological and Gnostic Chapters", in *The Practical and Theological Chapters and The Three Theological Discourses* (Kalamazoo, MI: Cistercian Publications, 1982), p. 70.

Taimni, Iqbal Kishen, *The Science of Yoga: The Yoga-Sūtras of Patañjali in Sanskrit with Transliteration in Roman, Translation in English, and Commentary* (Wheaton, IL: The Theosophical Publishing House, 1967).

Teresa of Avila, *The Book of Her Life*, tr. Kieran Kavanaugh and Otilio Rodriguez (Washington, DC: ICS Publications, 1976).

Teresa of Avila, "The Interior Castle", in *The Collected Works of St Teresa of Avila*, Vol. 2, tr. Kieran Kavanaugh and Otilio Rodriguez (Washington, DC: ICS Publications, 1980).

Teresa of Avila, *The Way of Perfection*, study edn, tr. Kieran Kavanaugh and Otilio Rodriguez (Washington, DC: ICS Publications, 2000).

Thérèse of Lisieux, *Story of a Soul: The Autobiography of St Thérèse of Lisieux*, third edn, tr. John Clarke, OCD (Washington, DC: ICS Publications, 1996).

Thomas Aquinas, *Summa Theologica Quaest. & Articul. Secundae Secundae Partis* (Rome: Forzani et Sodalis, 1928), pp. 588–90.

Thibodeaux, Mark E., SJ, *God's Voice Within: The Ignatian Way to Discover God's Will* (Chicago: Loyola Press, 2010).

Tsirpanlis, Constantine N., *Introduction to Eastern Patristic Thought and Orthodox Theology* (Collegeville, MN: Liturgical Press, 1991).

Tugwell, Simon, OP, *Ways of Imperfection: An Exploration of Christian Spirituality* (Springfield, IL: Templegate Publishers, 1985).

Tyler, Peter, *St John of the Cross* (London: Continuum, 2010).

Vaz, J. Clement, *Maranatha: Oriental Methods of Prayer and Meditation* (Bombay: St Paul's, 1990).

Vlachos, Hierotheos, *A Night in the Desert of the Holy Mountain: Discussion with a Hermit on the Jesus Prayer*, tr. Effie Mavromichali (Levadia, Greece: Birth of the Theotokos Monastery, 2009).

Ware, Kallistos, "Praying with the Body: The Hesychast Method and Non-Christian Parallels", *Sobornost, incorporating Eastern Churches Review* 14:2 (1992), pp. 6–35.

Ware, Kallistos, *The Jesus Prayer* (London: Catholic Truth Society, 2014).

Ware, Kallistos, *The Power of the Name* (Fairacres, Oxford: SLG Press, 1986).

Wellington, James F., *Christe Eleison! The Invocation of Christ in Eastern Monastic Psalmody c. 350–450* (Bern: Peter Lang, 2014).

Winston-Allen, Anne, *Stories of the Rose: The Making of the Rosary in the Middle Ages* (University Park, PA: The Pennsylvania State University Press, 1997).

Yogendra, Shri, *Yoga: Physical Education* (Santa Cruz, Bombay: The Yoga Institute, 1974).

Notes

1. Anonymous, *The Way of the Pilgrim and The Pilgrim Continues His Way*, tr. R. M. French (New York: Harper Collins, 1991).
2. *The Wisdom of Saint Isaac the Syrian,* tr. Sebastian Brock (Fairacres, Oxford: SLG Press, 1997), p. 18.
3. John L. McKenzie SJ, *Dictionary of the Bible* (London: Geoffrey Chapman, 1965), pp. 603–5.
4. Bruce M. Metzger & Michael D. Coogan (eds), *The Oxford Companion to the Bible* (Oxford: Oxford University Press, 1993), pp. 545–6.
5. McKenzie, *Dictionary of the Bible*, p. 604.
6. Mary Coloe, *God Dwells with Us: Temple Symbolism in the Fourth Gospel* (Collegeville, MN: Liturgical Press, 2001), pp. 42–3.
7. Antony F. Campbell SJ, *The Study Companion to Old Testament Literature: An Approach to the Writings of Pre-Exilic and Exilic Israel*, Old Testament Studies 2 (Wilmington, DL: Michael Glazier, 1989), pp. 159–60.
8. Kallistos Ware, *The Power of the Name: The Jesus Prayer in Orthodox Spirituality* (Fairacres, Oxford: SLG Press, 1986), pp. 12–13.
9. Ware, *The Power of the Name*, p. 11.
10. McKenzie, *Dictionary of the Bible*, pp. 604–5.
11. The imperative form *metanoiete* (repent) is in the imperfect tense, indicating an ongoing action.
12. *hypomonē*—the Greek word used here conveys the sense of "patient endurance".
13. St Gregory the Theologian, *Letter 80, To the Lawyer Eudoxios*, PG 37, 153C.
14. A Monk of Mount Athos, *The Watchful Mind: Teachings on the Prayer of the Heart,* tr. George Dokos (Yonkers, NY: St Vladimir's Seminary Press, 2014).
15. Thomas Aquinas, *Summa Theologica Quaest. & Articul. Secundae Partis.* (Rome: Forzani et Sodalis, 1928), pp. 588–90.
16. This is a reference to Hosea 6:6.

17. Per Olaf Sjogren, *The Jesus Prayer*, tr. Sydney Linton (London: SPCK, 1975), pp. 29–35.
18. *The Philokalia*, four vols, tr. G. E. H. Palmer, Philip Sherrard, and Kallistos Ware (London and Boston: Faber and Faber, 1979–95).
19. Jean-Claude Larchet, *Mental Disorders and Spiritual Healing: Teachings from the Early Christian East*, tr. Rama P. Coomaraswamy and G. John Champoux (Hillsdale, NY: Sophia Perennis, 2005), pp. 16–17.
20. St Irenaeus, *Against Heresies* II, 13, 3, tr. John Keble (Oxford: James Parker and Co., 1872), p. 123.
21. St Symeon the New Theologian, "Other Theological and Gnostic Chapters" in *The Practical and Theological Chapters & The Three Theological Discourses* (Kalamazoo, MI: Cistercian Publications, 1982), II, p. 70.
22. Evagrios the Solitary, "On Prayer: One Hundred and Fifty Three Texts", in *The Philokalia: The Complete Text*, Vol. 1, tr. and ed. G. E. H. Palmer, Philip Sherrard and Kallistos Ware (London: Faber and Faber, 1990), p. 63.
23. St Maximus the Confessor, "On the Beginning and End of Rational Creatures", *PG*, Vol. 91, 1100AB.
24. Larchet, *Mental Disorders and Spiritual Healing*, p. 22.
25. St Maximus, "Third Century on Love", in *The Philokalia*, Vol. 2, No. 32, p. 88.
26. St Gregory of Nyssa, *On the Soul and the Resurrection*, tr. Catharine P. Roth (Crestwood, NY: St Vladimir's Seminary Press, 1993), p. 68.
27. St John of Damascus, *On the Orthodox Faith*, PG 94, 928 BC.
28. St Athanasius, *Against the Heathen*, PG 25, 65B.
29. Jean-Claude Larchet, *Mental Disorders and Spiritual Healing: Teachings from the Early Christian East*, tr. Rama Coomaraswamy and G. John Champoux (Hillsdale, NY: Sophia Perennis, 2005), p. 30.
30. Archbishop Chrysostomos, *A Guide to Orthodox Psychotherapy: The Science, Theology, and Spiritual Practice Behind It and Its Clinical Applications* (Lanham, MD: University Press of America, 2007), pp. 36–7.
31. Larchet, *Mental Disorders and Spiritual Healing*, pp. 27–8.
32. Frederick William Danker (ed.), *A Greek–English Lexicon of the New Testament and other Early Christian Literature* (Chicago: University of Chicago Press, 2000), pp. 1098–1100.
33. Mark A. House (ed.), *Compact Greek–English Lexicon of the New Testament* (Peabody, MA: Hendrickson Publishers, 2008), p. 190.
34. House (ed.) *Compact Greek-English Lexicon*, pp. 139–40.

35. Danker, *Greek-English Lexicon*, pp. 832-6.
36. Danker, *Greek-English Lexicon*, p. 680.
37. St John of Damascus, *On the Orthodox Faith*, PG 94, 924 B.
38. Vladimir Lossky, *The Mystical Theology of the Eastern Church* (Crestwood, NY: St Vladimir's Seminary Press, 1976), p. 201.
39. Larchet, *Mental Disorders and Spiritual Healing*, p. 31.
40. Jean-Yves Leloup, *Being Still: Reflections on an Ancient Mystical Tradition*, tr. and ed. M. S. Laird (Mahwah, NJ: Paulist Press, 2003), p. 123.
41. *The Philokalia*, Vol 1, pp. 361-2.
42. Gregory Palamas, "Homily Thirty One", in *The Homilies*, tr. and ed. Christopher Veniamin (Waymart, PA: Mount Thabor Publishing, 2009), pp. 243-50.
43. Archbishop Chrysostomos, *A Guide to Orthodox Psychotherapy*, p. 46.
44. St John of Damascus, *On the Orthodox Faith*, PG 94, 924A.
45. Athanasius, *On the Incarnation*, PG 25, 192B, *"autos gar enenthropesen hina hemeis theopoiethomen"*.
46. St John of Damascus, *On the Orthodox Faith*, PG 94, 798 B.
47. Athanasius, *On the Incarnation*, PG 25, 17, 125B, *"kai hosper en pasē tē ktisei on, ektos men esti tou pantos kat'ousiav, en pasi de esti tais eautou dynamei"*.
48. Ken Parry et al. (eds), *Blackwell Dictionary of Eastern Christianity* (Oxford: Blackwell Publishers, 1997), pp. 230-1.
49. Constantine N. Tsirpanlis, *Introduction to Eastern Patristic Thought and Orthodox Theology* (Collegeville, MN: Liturgical Press, 1991), p. 7.
50. *The Ascetic Homilies of Saint Isaac the Syrian*, Homily 65 (Boston, MA: Holy Transfiguration Monastery, 2011), p. 465.
51. Fr George Habra, "The Sources of the Doctrine of Gregory Palamas on the Divine Energies", *Eastern Churches Quarterly* 12:6 (1957-8), p. 245.
52. Archbishop Chrysostomos, *A Guide to Orthodox Psychotherapy*, pp. 80-1.
53. Archbishop Chrysostomos, *A Guide to Orthodox Psychotherapy*, pp. 82-3.
54. John Meyendorff, *St Gregory Palamas and Orthodox Spirituality* (Crestwood, NY: St Vladimir's Seminary Press, 1974), pp. 121-3.
55. Joseph Raya, *The Face of God* (Denville, NJ: Dimension Books, 1976), pp. 37-8.
56. Archbishop Chrysostomos, *A Guide to Orthodox Psychotherapy*, p. 89.
57. Archbishop Chrysostomos, *A Guide to Orthodox Psychotherapy*, pp. 89-95.
58. Meyendorff, *St Gregory Palamas and Orthodox Spirituality*, pp. 102-3.

59. Meyendorff, *St Gregory Palamas and Orthodox Spirituality*, p. 103.
60. Meyendorff, *St Gregory Palamas and Orthodox Spirituality*, p. 107.
61. St Gregory Palamas, *The Triads*, tr. Nicholas Gendle (Mahwah, NJ: Paulist Press, 1983), p. 51.
62. Meyendorff, *St Gregory Palamas and Orthodox Spirituality*, pp. 109–11.
63. A Priest of the Byzantine Church, *Reflections on the Jesus Prayer: A Phrase by Phrase Analysis of "The Prayer of the Heart"* (Denville, NJ: Dimension Books, 1978), pp. 21–2.
64. A Priest of the Byzantine Church, *Reflections on the Jesus* Prayer, p. 22.
65. John S. Romanides, *Patristic Theology: The University Lectures of Fr John Romanides* (Thessaloniki, Greece: Uncut Mountain Press, 2008), p. 38.
66. Romanides, *Patristic Theology*, p. 48.
67. Romanides, *Patristic Theology*, p. 58.
68. Romanides, *Patristic Theology*, p. 204.
69. Boniface Ramsey, *Beginning to Read the Fathers, Revised edition* (Mahwah, NJ: Paulist Press, 2012), pp. 174–93.
70. St Augustine, "Discourse on Psalm 37", in *Enarrationes in Psalmos*, Vol 2, tr. Scholastica Hebgin and Felicitas Corrigan (London: Green and Co., 1961), p. 344.
71. St Augustine, "Letter to Proba", in *Letters of St Augustine of Hippo*, tr. J. G. Cunningham (Edinburgh: T&T Clark, 1875), pp. 155–6.
72. Ware, *The Power of the Name*, p. 13.
73. Irénée Hausherr, *The Name of Jesus* (Collegeville, MN: Liturgical Press–Cistercian Publications, 2008), p. 9.
74. Hausherr, *The Name of Jesus*, pp. 194–200.
75. Hausherr, *The Name of Jesus*, p. 198.
76. Hausherr, *The Name of Jesus*, p. 200.
77. Hausherr, *The Name of Jesus*, pp. 201–4.
78. Hausherr, *The Name of Jesus*, p. 53.
79. Hausherr, *The Name of Jesus*, p. 119.
80. David Hester, *The Jesus Prayer: A Gift from the Fathers* (Ben Lomond, CA: Conciliar Press, 2001), pp. 9–10.
81. Evagrios the Solitary, *On Prayer*, PG 79, 1181C.
82. Hausherr, *The Name of Jesus*, p. 157.
83. Hausherr, *The Name of Jesus*, p. 214.
84. Hausherr, *The Name of Jesus*, pp. 173–4.

85. Hester, *The Jesus Prayer*, p. 8.
86. Pseudo Macarius, "Homily 15. 20" in *The Fifty Spiritual Homilies and The Great Letter*, tr. George A. Maloney (New York: Paulist Press, 1992), p. 116.
87. Antoine Guillamont, "The Jesus Prayer among the Monks of Egypt", *Eastern Churches Review* 6 (1974), p. 70.
88. Guillamont, "The Jesus Prayer among the Monks of Egypt", pp. 67–9.
89. Guillamont, "The Jesus Prayer among the Monks of Egypt", p. 69.
90. Guillamont, "The Jesus Prayer among the Monks of Egypt", p. 70.
91. Hausherr, *The Name of Jesus*, p. 104.
92. St John Cassian, *Conferences*, tr. Colm Luibheid (Mahwah, NJ: Paulist Press, 1985).
93. Cassian, *Conferences*, p. 111.
94. Cassian, *Conferences*, p. 124.
95. Cassian, *Conferences*, p. 131.
96. Cassian, *Conferences*, p. 132.
97. Cassian, *Conferences*, p. 133.
98. Cassian, *Conferences*, pp. 135–6.
99. Cassian, *Conferences*, p. 138.
100. Cassian, *Conferences*, p. 139.
101. Cassian, *Conferences*, p. 139.
102. Hausherr, *The Name of Jesus*, pp. 242–3.
103. Hausherr, *The Name of Jesus*, pp. 246–51.
104. Hausherr, *The Name of Jesus*, pp. 214–20.
105. Hausherr, *The Name of Jesus*, p. 225.
106. Hester, *The Jesus Prayer*, p. 11.
107. Diadochos of Photike, "On Spiritual Knowledge and Discrimination" in *The Philokalia*, Vol. 1, p. 285.
108. Kallistos Ware, *The Jesus Prayer* (London: Catholic Truth Society, 2014), pp. 8–9.
109. Diadochus of Photike, "On Spiritual Knowledge and Discrimination", p. 270.
110. Hausherr, *The Name of Jesus*, p. 267.
111. Hausherr, *The Name of Jesus*, pp. 267–70.
112. Hester, *The Jesus Prayer*, p. 11.
113. "A Discourse on Abba Philimon" in *The Philokalia*, Vol. 2, p. 347.
114. "A Discourse on Abba Philimon" in *The Philokalia*, Vol. 2, p. 348.

[115] John Climacus, *The Ladder of Divine Ascent*, tr. Colm Luibheid and Norman Russell (Mahwah, NJ: Paulist Press, 1982).
[116] Climacus, *The Ladder of Divine Ascent*, p. 200.
[117] Climacus, *The Ladder of Divine Ascent*, p. 270.
[118] Climacus, *The Ladder of Divine Ascent*, p. 275.
[119] Climacus, *The Ladder of Divine Ascent*, p. 276.
[120] Hester, *The Jesus Prayer*, p. 13.
[121] Hesychios the Priest, "On Watchfulness and Holiness", in *The Philokalia*, Vol. 1, p. 197.
[122] Ware, *The Power of the Name*, p. 1.
[123] David J. Melling, "Hesychasm", in Parry, Ken et al. (eds), *The Blackwell Dictionary of Eastern Christianity* (Oxford: Blackwell Publishers, 1999) p. 230.
[124] A Monk of the Eastern Church (Lev Gillet), *The Jesus Prayer* (Crestwood, NY: St Vladimir's Seminary Press, 1987), pp. 53–4.
[125] Archbishop Chrysostomos, *A Guide to Orthodox Psychotherapy: The Science, Theology, and Spiritual Practice Behind It and Its Clinical Application* (Lanham, MD: University Press of America, 2007).
[126] Hester, *The Jesus Prayer*, p. 17.
[127] Nikiphoros The Monk, "On Watchfulness and the Guarding of the Heart", in *The Philokalia*, Vol. 4, pp. 205–6.
[128] Ware, *The Power of the Name*, p. 27.
[129] Hester, *The Jesus Prayer*, p. 24.
[130] Hester, *The Jesus Prayer*, p. 26.
[131] Hester, *The Jesus Prayer*, pp. 26–7.
[132] Anonymous, *The Way of the Pilgrim and The Pilgrim Continues His Way*, tr. R. M. French (New York: Harper Collins Publishers, 1991).
[133] Ware, *The Power of the Name*, p. 29.
[134] Rama Coomaraswamy, *The Invocation of the Name of Jesus: As Practiced in the Western Church* (Louisville, KY: Fons Vitae, 1999), p. 7.
[135] Anne Winston-Allen, *Stories of the Rose: The Making of the Rosary in the Middle Ages* (University Park, PA: Pennsylvania State University Press, 1997).
[136] Winston-Allen, *Stories of the Rose*, p. 2.
[137] Winston-Allen, *Stories of the Rose*, pp. 13–30.
[138] Arthur L. Basham, *The Wonder that was India* (New Delhi: Rupa & Co., 1994), pp. 325–8.

139 J. Clement Vaz, *Oriental Methods of Prayer and Meditation* (Bombay: St Pauls, 1990), p. 23.
140 Gerhard Oberhammer, "The Use of Mantra in Yogic Meditation: The Testimony of the Pāśupata", in Alper, Harvey P. (ed.), *Understanding Mantras* (Albany, NY: State University of New York Press, 1989), p. 204.
141 Yoga Sutra 1:23 *"Īśvara-praṇidhānād vā.* My translations have been used for all the Yoga Sutras quoted in this chapter.
142 Sutra 1:24 *Kleśa-karma-vipākāśayair aparāmṛṣṭaḥ puruṣa-viśeṣa Īshvaraḥ.*
143 Sutra 1:25 *Tatra niratiśayaṃ Sarvajña-bījam.*
144 Sutra 1:26 *Sa pūrveṣām api guruḥ kālenāna-vacchedāt.*
145 Sutra 1:27 *Tasya vācakaḥ praṇavaḥ.*
146 Sutra 1:28 *Tajjapas tad-artha-bhāvanam.*
147 Sutra 1:29 *Tataḥ pratyak-cetanādhigamo 'py antarāyā-bhāvaś ca.*
148 Basham, *The Wonder that was India*, p. 328.
149 Sutra 1:2 *Yogaś citta-vṛtti-nirodhaḥ.*
150 Sutra II:46 *Sthira-sukham āsanam.*
151 Shri Yogendra, *Yoga: Physical Education* (Santa Cruz, Bombay: The Yoga Institute, 1974), p. 127.
152 Yogendra, *Yoga: Physical Education*, p. 128.
153 Sutra IV:1 *The siddhis are acquired as a result of one's birth, drugs, recitation of mantras, performing austerities or achieving samādhi.*
154 Sutra III:38 *These powers are obstacles in the way of samādhi when (the mind is) turned outward.*
155 Jan Gonda, "The Indian Mantra", *Oriens* 16 (1963), p. 246.
156 Mark Gwynn and Amanda Laugesen (eds), *The Australian Concise Oxford Dictionary of Current English*, sixth edn (Melbourne: Oxford University Press, 2017), p. 864.
157 Harold Coward and David Goa, *Mantra: Hearing the Divine in India* (Chambersburg, PA: Anima Books, 1991), p. 3.
158 Gonda, "The Indian Mantra", p. 257.
159 Gonda, "The Indian Mantra", p. 284.
160 Coward and Goa, *Mantra*, p. 11.
161 André Padoux, "Mantras—What Are They?", in Alper, Harvey P. (ed.), *Understanding Mantras* (Albany, NY: State University of New York Press, 1989), p. 297.
162 Coward and Goa, *Mantra*, pp. 14–15.

163 Coward and Goa, *Mantra*, p. 22.
164 Coward and Goa, *Mantra*, p. 39.
165 I. K. Taimni, *The Science of Yoga: The Yoga-Sūtras of Patañjali in Sanskrit with Transliteration in Roman, Translation in English and Commentary* (Wheaton, IL: The Theosophical Publishing House, 1967), pp. 63–73.
166 Mircea Eliade, *Yoga: Immortality and Freedom* (Princeton, NJ: Princeton University Press, 1969), pp. 212–14.
167 Coward and Goa, *Mantra*, pp. 42–4.
168 Padoux, "Mantras—What Are They?", pp. 298–302.
169 Shauna L. Shapiro, Roger Walsh and Willoughby B. Britton, "An Analysis of Recent Meditation Research and Suggestions for Future Directions", *Journal for Meditation and Meditation Research* 3 (2003), p. 70.
170 Michael Delmonte and Vincent Kenny, "Models of Meditation", *British Journal of Psychotherapy* 1:3 (1985), pp. 197–214.
171 Michael McGee, "Meditation and Psychiatry", *Psychiatry* 5(1), (January 2008), pp. 28–40.
172 Cynthia Bourgeault, *Centering Prayer and Inner Awakening* (Lanham, MD: Cowley Publications, 2004), p. 20.
173 Michael McGee, "Meditation and Psychiatry", *Psychiatry* 5(1), (January 2008), pp. 28–40.
174 Daniel Goleman and Richard J. Davidson, *The Science of Meditation: How to Change Your Brain, Mind and Body* (London: Penguin Random House, 2017), p. 14.
175 Goleman and Davidson, *The Science of Meditation*, pp. 165–248.
176 H. J. H. Kuijpers, F. M. M. A. van der Heijden, S. Tuinier and W. M. A. Verhoeven, "Meditation Induced Psychosis", *Psychopathology* 40 (2007), pp. 461–4.
177 Arthur A. Lazarus, "Psychiatric Problems Precipitated by Transcendental Meditation", *Psychological Reports* (1976), pp. 601–2.
178 Jean-Marie Déchanet, *Christian Yoga* (London: Burns & Oates, 1960).
179 Déchanet, *Christian Yoga*, p. 3.
180 Déchanet, *Christian Yoga*, p. 15.
181 Déchanet, *Christian Yoga*, p. 17.
182 Déchanet, *Christian Yoga*, pp. 128–30.
183 J. Clement Vaz, *Maranatha: Oriental Methods of Prayer and Meditation* (Bombay: St Paul's, 1990), p. 23.

184 Thomas Ryan, *Prayer of Heart and Body: Meditation and Yoga as Christian Spiritual Practice* (Mahwah, NJ: Paulist Press, 1995), p. 21.
185 Ryan, *Prayer of Heart and Body*, pp. 28–9.
186 Ryan, *Prayer of Heart and Body*, p. 63.
187 Ryan, *Prayer of Heart and Body*, p. 64.
188 Ryan, *Prayer of Heart and Body*, p. 217.
189 Thomas Matus, *Yoga and the Jesus Prayer Tradition: An Experiment in Faith* (Mahwah, NJ: Paulist Press, 1984), p. 4.
190 Matus, *Yoga and the Jesus Prayer Tradition*, p. 8.
191 Matus, *Yoga and the Jesus Prayer Tradition*, p. 155.
192 Matus, *Yoga and the Jesus Prayer Tradition*, pp. 153–5.
193 Anthony de Mello, SJ, *Sadhana: A Way to God. Christian Exercises in Eastern Form* (New York: Image Books, Doubleday, 1984), pp. 13–61.
194 de Mello, *Sadhana*, pp. 29–30.
195 de Mello, *Sadhana*, pp. 30–6.
196 de Mello, *Sadhana*, p. 110.
197 de Mello, *Sadhana*, p. 112.
198 de Mello, *Sadhana*, pp. 122–3.
199 de Mello, *Sadhana*, p. 119.
200 Kallistos Ware, "Praying with the Body: The Hesychast Method and Non-Christian Parallels", *Sobornost* 12:2 (1992), pp. 6–35.
201 Ware, "Praying with the Body", p. 10.
202 Gabriel Bungé, *Earthen Vessels: The Practice of Personal Prayer According to the Patristic Tradition*, tr. Michael J. Miller (San Francisco: Ignatius Press, 2002), pp. 141–8.
203 Ware, "Praying with the Body", pp. 16–17.
204 Ware, "Praying with the Body", p. 19.
205 Ware, "Praying with the Body", p. 21.
206 Anthony Bloom, *Asceticism (Somatopsychic Techniques in Greek Orthodox Christianity)*, Guild Lecture No. 95, (London: The Guild of Pastoral Psychology, 1957), p. 11.
207 Bloom, *Asceticism*, pp. 12–16.
208 Bloom, *Ascetisism*, p. 15.
209 Gillet, *The Jesus Prayer*, p. 74.
210 Ware, "Praying with the Body", p. 29.
211 Ware, "Praying with the Body", pp. 30–1.

212. John R. Dupuche, "Sufism and Hesychasm", in Bronwen Neil, Geoffrey D. Dunn and Lawrence Cross (eds), *Prayer and Spirituality in the Early Church*, Volume 3: Liturgy and Life (Strathfield, NSW: St Paul Publications, 2003), pp. 335-44.
213. Dupuche, "Sufism and Hesychasm", p. 343.
214. *The Rule of St Basil in Latin and English*, tr. Anna M. Silvas (Collegeville, MN: Liturgical Press, 2013), pp. 71-3.
215. Jacques-Albert Cuttat, *The Encounter of Religions: A Dialogue between the West and the Orient with an Essay on the Prayer of Jesus* (New York: Desclée Company, 1960), p. 90.
216. William Johnston SJ, *Mystical Theology: The Science of Love* (London: Harper Collins, 1995), pp. 62-4.
217. Tim Peeters, *When Silence Speaks: The Spiritual Way of the Carthusian Order* (London: Darton, Longman and Todd, 2015), p. 64.
218. Peeters, *When Silence Speaks*, p. 98.
219. Bourgeault, *Centering Prayer and Inner Awakening*, pp. 66-8.
220. Columba Stewart OSB, *Cassian the Monk* (New York: Oxford University Press, 1998), pp. 112-13.
221. Bourgeault, *Centering Prayer and Inner Awakening*, pp. 70-1.
222. Thomas Ryan, *Prayer of the Heart and Body: Meditation and Yoga as Christian Spiritual Practice* (Mahwah, NJ: Paulist Press, 1995), p. 39.
223. William Johnston, Introduction to *The Cloud of Unknowing and The Book of Privy Counseling* (New York: Image Books, 1973), pp. 24-7.
224. Pseudo-Dionysius, "The Mystical Theology" in *Pseudo-Dionysius: The Complete Works*. tr. Colm Luibheid (Mahwah, NJ: Paulist Press, 1987), p. 135.
225. Johnston, Introduction to *The Cloud of Unknowing*, pp. 28-30.
226. *The Cloud of Unknowing*, tr. William Johnston (New York: Image Books, 1973), p. 35.
227. *The Cloud of Unknowing*, p. 35.
228. *The Cloud of Unknowing*, p. 36.
229. *The Cloud of Unknowing*, p. 36.
230. *The Cloud of Unknowing*, pp. 131-2.
231. *The Cloud of Unknowing*, pp. 132-4.
232. *The Cloud of Unknowing*, p. 75.
233. *The Cloud of Unknowing*, p. 75.
234. *The Cloud of Unknowing*, p. 76.

[235] *The Cloud of Unknowing*, p. 37.
[236] *The Cloud of Unknowing*, p. 39.
[237] *The Cloud of Unknowing*, p. 40.
[238] *The Cloud of Unknowing*, p. 42.
[239] *The Cloud of Unknowing*, p. 45.
[240] *The Cloud of Unknowing*, p. 46.
[241] *The Cloud of Unknowing*, p. 46.
[242] *The Cloud of Unknowing*, p. 48.
[243] *The Cloud of Unknowing*, p. 48.
[244] *The Cloud of Unknowing*, p. 51.
[245] *The Cloud of Unknowing*, p. 78.
[246] *The Cloud of Unknowing*, p. 73.
[247] *The Cloud of Unknowing*, p. 80.
[248] *The Cloud of Unknowing*, p. 81.
[249] *The Cloud of Unknowing*, pp. 82-3.
[250] *The Cloud of Unknowing*, p. 83.
[251] *The Cloud of Unknowing*, p. 83.
[252] *The Cloud of Unknowing*, p. 85.
[253] *The Cloud of Unknowing*, p. 85.
[254] *The Cloud of Unknowing*, pp. 91-2.
[255] *The Cloud of Unknowing*, p. 101.
[256] *The Cloud of Unknowing*, p. 124.
[257] *The Cloud of Unknowing*, p. 127.
[258] *The Cloud of Unknowing*, p. 51.
[259] Simon Tugwell OP, *Ways of Imperfection: An Exploration of Christian Spirituality* (Springfield, IL: Templegate Publishers, 1985), p. 176.
[260] Paul Harris (ed.), *John Main: A Biography in Text and Photos* (Catalina, AZ: Medio Media Publishing, 2001), pp. 3-10.
[261] Harris, *John Main*, pp. 12-13.
[262] Harris, *John Main*, p. 16.
[263] Harris, *John Main*, pp. 17-18.
[264] John Main, *Christian Meditation: The Gethsemani Talks* (Tucson, AZ: Medio Media Publishing, 2001), p. 13.
[265] Main, *Christian Meditation*, p. 14.
[266] Main, *Christian Meditation*, p. 28.
[267] Main, *Christian Meditation*, pp. 30-1.

268 Timothy Fry OSB (ed.), *The Rule of St Benedict* (Collegeville, MN: Liturgical Press, 1982), chapters 42 and 73.
269 Fry, *The Rule of St Benedict*, p. 52.
270 John Main, *The Inner Christ* (London: Darton, Longman and Todd, 1987), p. vi.
271 John Main, *Word into Silence* (Norwich: Canterbury Press 2006), p. x.
272 Main, *Word into Silence*, p. 1.
273 Main, *Word into Silence*, p. 3.
274 Main, *Word into Silence*, p. 7.
275 Main, *Word into Silence*, p. 9.
276 Main, *Word into Silence*, p. 9.
277 Main, *Word into Silence*, p. 10.
278 Cassian, PL 49, 10.11, 837A.
279 Main, *Word into Silence*, pp. 10–11.
280 Main, *Word into Silence*, pp. 12–16.
281 Main, *Word into Silence*, pp. 26–7.
282 Main, *Word into Silence*, pp. 44–5.
283 Main, *Word into Silence*, p. 48.
284 Main, *Word into Silence*, pp. 52–3.
285 Main, *Word into Silence*, p. 54.
286 Main, *Word into Silence*, pp. 69–73.
287 John Main, *Christian Meditation*.
288 Augustine Baker, *Holy Wisdom or Directions for the Prayer of Contemplation* (London: Burns & Oates, 2011).
289 Main, *Christian Meditation*, pp. 16–18.
290 Main, *Christian Meditation*, pp. 27–33.
291 Main, *Christian Meditation*, pp. 38–9.
292 John Main, *Moment of Christ* (London: Darton, Longman and Todd, 1987), pp. 102–4.
293 Bourgeault, *Centering Prayer and Inner Awakening*, pp. 63–4.
294 Bourgeault, *Centering Prayer and Inner Awakening*, p. 64.
295 Main, *Christian Meditation*, pp. 38–9.
296 Bourgeault, *Centering Prayer and Inner Awakening*, pp. 20–3.
297 M. Basil Pennington, *Centering Prayer: Renewing an Ancient Christian Prayer Form* (New York: Image, Doubleday, 2001), p. xvi.

298 Thomas Keating, *Invitation to Love: The Way of Christian Contemplation* (London: Bloomsbury, 2011), pp. 1–2.
299 Bourgeault, *Centering Prayer and Inner Awakening*, pp. 57–8.
300 Pennington, *Centering Prayer* (Garden City, NY: Doubleday, 1980).
301 Pennington, *Centering Prayer*, pp. 120–2.
302 Thomas Keating, *Open Mind, Open Heart: The Contemplative Dimension of the Gospel*, 20th Anniversary Edition (New York, Continuum, 2006), p. 178.
303 Keating, *Open Mind, Open Heart*, p. 12.
304 Keating, *Open Mind, Open Heart*, p. 33.
305 Keating, *Open Mind, Open Heart*, p. 41.
306 Keating, *Open Mind, Open Heart*, p. 80.
307 Keating, *Open Mind, Open Heart*, p. 81.
308 Keating, *Open Mind, Open Heart*, pp. 95–8.
309 Keating, *Open Mind, Open Heart*, p. 99.
310 Thomas Keating, *The Mystery of Christ: The Liturgy as Spiritual Experience* (New York: Continuum International Publishing Group Inc, 1987), pp. 1–12.
311 American Psychiatric Association, *Diagnostic and Statistical Manual of Mental Disorders, (DSM-5)* (5th edn, Arlington, VA: American Psychiatric Publishing, 2013), pp. 644–84.
312 Keating, *Invitation to Love*, p. 6.
313 Keating, *Invitation to Love*, p. 15.
314 Keating, *Invitation to Love*, p. 19.
315 Keating, *Invitation to Love*, p. 27.
316 Bourgeault, *Centering Prayer and Inner Awakening*, p. 12.
317 Bourgeault, *Centering Prayer and Inner Awakening*, pp. 31–2.
318 Bourgeault, *Centering Prayer and Inner Awakening*, pp. 80–8.
319 Bourgeault, *Centering Prayer and Inner Awakening*, pp. 101–4.
320 William A. Meninger OCSO, *The Loving Search for God: Contemplative Prayer in the Cloud of Unknowing* (New York: Continuum, 2012), p. xvii.
321 Basil Pennington OCSO, *Centering Prayer: Renewing an Ancient Christian Prayer Form* (New York: Image Books, 2001).
322 Smith, Foreword to *The Cloud of Unknowing*, p. 36.
323 Keating, *Open Mind, Open Heart*, p. 2.
324 Pennington, *Centering Prayer*, pp. 23–5.
325 Pennington, *Centering Prayer*, p. 25.

326 Keith J. Egan, "The Solitude of Carmelite Prayer", in Egan, Keith J. (ed.), *Carmelite Prayer: A Tradition for the 21st Century* (Mahwah, NJ: Paulist Press, 2003), pp. 38–60.
327 Egan, "The Solitude of Carmelite Prayer", p. 43.
328 Ernest Larkin, "The Carmelite Tradition and Centering Prayer/Christian Meditation", in Egan, Keith J. (ed.), *Carmelite Prayer: A Tradition for the 21st Century* (Mahwah, NJ: Paulist Press, 2003), p. 209.
329 Egan, "Carmelite Prayer", p. 45.
330 Larkin, "Carmelite Tradition", p. 211.
331 Brother Lawrence of the Resurrection, "The Practice of the Presence of God", in *Writings and Conversations On the Practice of the Presence of God*, tr. Salvatore Sciurba OCD (Washington, DC: Institute of Carmelite Studies, 1994), pp. 105–8.
332 St Thérèse of Lisieux, *Story of A Soul: The Autobiography of Saint Thérèse of Lisieux*, tr. John Clarke OCD (Washington, DC: ICS Publications, 1996), p. 188.
333 St Thérèse of Lisieux, *Story of A Soul*, p. 179.
334 Mark O'Keefe, *The Way of Transformation: Saint Teresa of Avila on the Foundation and Fruit of Prayer* (Washington, DC: ICS Publications, 2016), pp. 14–27.
335 O'Keefe, *The Way of Transformation*, pp. 21–2.
336 Teresa of Avila, "The Interior Castle", in *The Collected Works of St Teresa of Avila*, Vol. 2, tr. Kieran Kavanaugh OCD and Otilio Rodriguez OCD (Washington, DC: ICS Publications, 2000), p. 319.
337 Teresa of Avila, *The Interior Castle*, p. 446.
338 O'Keefe, *The Way of Transformation*, p. 44.
339 Teresa of Avila, *The Way of Perfection*, tr. Kieran Kavanaugh OCD and Otilio Rodriguez OCD (Washington, DC: ICS Publications, 2000), p. 229.
340 O'Keefe, *The Way of Transformation*, p. 68.
341 Teresa of Avila, *The Interior Castle*, p. 447.
342 Teresa of Avila, *The Way of Perfection*, p. 431.
343 Teresa of Avila, *The Way of Perfection*, p. 401.
344 Teresa of Avila, *The Way of Perfection*, pp. 370, 372.
345 Teresa of Avila, *The Interior Castle*, p. 420.
346 Teresa of Avila, *The Way of Perfection*, p. 123.
347 Teresa of Avila, *The Interior Castle*, p. 445.

[348] Teresa of Avila, *The Way of Perfection*, p. 330.
[349] Teresa of Avila, *The Book of Her Life* (Washington, DC: ICS Publications, 1976), p. 96.
[350] Teresa of Avila, *The Way of Perfection*, pp. 261–2.
[351] O'Keefe, *The Way of Transformation*, p. 46.
[352] Teresa of Avila, *The Way of Perfection*, p. 300.
[353] Teresa of Avila, *The Way of Perfection*, pp. 277–321.
[354] Kieran Kavanaugh OCD, "Contemplation and the Stream of Consciousness", in Egan, Keith J. (ed.), *Carmelite Prayer: A Tradition for the 21st Century* (Mahwah, NJ: Paulist Press, 2003), pp. 102–4.
[355] Teresa of Avila, *The Way of Perfection*, p. 277.
[356] Teresa of Avila, *The Way of Perfection*, p. 278.
[357] O'Keefe, *The Way of Transformation*, p. 48.
[358] Teresa of Avila, *The Way of Perfection*, p. 300.
[359] Teresa of Avila, *The Way of Perfection*, p. 171.
[360] Larkin, "Carmelite Tradition", p. 215.
[361] Larkin, "Carmelite Tradition", pp. 202–3.
[362] Larkin, "Carmelite Tradition", p. 203.
[363] James Arraj, *From St John of the Cross to Us: The Story of a 400 Year Long Misunderstanding and What it Means for the Future of Christian Mysticism* (Chiloquin, OR: Inner Growth Books, 1999), pp. 1–14.
[364] Kevin Culligan OCD, "The Dark Night and Depression", in Egan, Keith J. (ed.), *Carmelite Prayer: A Tradition for the 21st Century*, (Mahwah, NJ: Paulist Press, 2003), pp. 122–6.
[365] Peter Tyler, *St John of the Cross* (London: Continuum, 2010), p. 2.
[366] Tyler, *St John of the Cross*, p. 86.
[367] St John of the Cross, "The Dark Night", in *The Collected Works of St John of the Cross*, tr. K. Kavanaugh and O. Rodriguez (Washington, DC: Institute of Carmelite Studies, 1973), p. 295.
[368] Gerald G. May, *The Dark Night of the Soul: A Psychiatrist Explores the Connection between Darkness and Spiritual Growth* (New York: Harper San Francisco, 2005), p. 67.
[369] St John of the Cross, *The Dark Night*, pp. 295–6.
[370] St John of the Cross, "Maxims on Love", in *The Collected Works of St John of the Cross*, p. 678.
[371] Keating, *Invitation to Love*, pp. 100–1.

[372] St John of the Cross, *The Dark Night*, p. 313.
[373] St John of the Cross, *The Dark Night*, p. 315.
[374] St John of the Cross, *The Dark Night*, pp. 327-8.
[375] St John of the Cross, *The Dark Night*, p. 328.
[376] May, *Dark Night of the Soul*, pp. 142-9.
[377] *The Carmelite Directory of the Spiritual Life* (ET: Chicago, IL: Carmelite Press, 1951), p. 546.
[378] St John of the Cross, *The Dark Night*, p. 335.
[379] Culligan, "Dark Night and Depression", pp. 130-5.
[380] Culligan, "Dark Night and Depression", p. 131.
[381] Teresa of Avila, *The Way of Perfection*, p. 464.
[382] St John of the Cross, *The Ascent of Mount Carmel*, pp. 289-90.
[383] St John of the Cross, *The Ascent of Mount Carmel*, p. 181.
[384] Teresa of Avila, *The Interior Castle*, p. 399.
[385] Teresa of Avila, *The Way of Perfection*, p. 278.
[386] Teresa of Avila, *The Way of Perfection*, p. 181.
[387] Brother Lawrence of the Resurrection, "Spiritual Maxims", in *Writings and Conversations On the Practice of the Presence of God*, tr. Salvatore Sciurba OCD (Washington, DC: Institute of Carmelite Studies, 1994).
[388] Brother Lawrence of the Resurrection, "Spiritual Maxims", pp. 35-44.
[389] Venard Poslusney OCarm, *Prayer, Aspiration and Contemplation* (New York: Alba House, 1975), p. 67.
[390] Avery Dulles SJ, in *The Spiritual Exercises of St Ignatius* (New York: Vintage Books, 2000), pp. xiii-xx.
[391] Ignatius of Loyola, *Personal Writings: Reminiscences, Spiritual Diary, Select Letters, including the text of The Spiritual Exercises*, tr. Joseph A. Munitiz and Philip Endean (London: Penguin Books, 1996), p. 13.
[392] Ignatius of Loyola, *Personal Writings*, p. 22.
[393] Ignatius of Loyola, *Personal Writings*, p. 25.
[394] Ignatius of Loyola, *Personal Writings*, p. 27.
[395] Dulles, in *The Spiritual Exercises of St Ignatius*, pp. xix-xx.
[396] *The Spiritual Exercises of St Ignatius Loyola,* tr. Michael Ivens SJ (London: Gracewing, 2004), Annotation 1, p. 1.
[397] *The Spiritual Exercises of St Ignatius Loyola*, Annotation 1, p. 1.

398 Michael Ivens SJ, *Understanding the Spiritual Exercises: Text and Commentary—A Handbook for Retreat Directors* (Leominster, Herefordshire: Gracewing, 1998), p. 53.
399 Ivens, *Understanding the Spiritual Exercises*, pp. 33–4.
400 Ivens, *Understanding the Spiritual Exercises*, pp. 205–37.
401 *The Spiritual Exercises of St Ignatius Loyola*, p. 94.
402 Examples are: Mark E. Thibodeaux, *God's Voice Within: The Ignatian Way to Discover God's Will* (Chicago: Loyola Press, 2010) and Timothy Gallagher, *The Discernment of Spirits* (New York: Crossroads, 2005).
403 Ivens, *Understanding the Spiritual Exercises*, pp. 70–5.
404 Ivens, *Understanding the Spiritual Exercises*, p. 70.
405 Ivens, *Understanding the Spiritual Exercises*, p. 74.
406 Mother Maria, *The Jesus Prayer: The Meeting of East and West in the Prayer of the Heart* (Newport Pagnell, Buckinghamshire: Lovat Press, 1972), p. 3.
407 Ware, *The Power of the Name*, p. 4.
408 Lev Gillet (A Monk of the Eastern Church), *On the Invocation of the Name of Jesus* (Springfield, IL: Templegate Publishers, 1985), p. 28.
409 Ware, *The Power of the Name*, p. 6.
410 Placide Deseille, "The Hesychast Prayer in the Orthodox Church", in Coomaraswamy, Rama, *The Invocation of the Name of Jesus: As Practiced in the Western Church* (Louisville, KY: Fons Vitae, 1999), p. 243.
411 Sophrony Sakharov, *On Prayer* (Crestwood, NY: St Vladimir's Seminary Press, 1998), p. 167.
412 Sakharov, *On Prayer*, p. 156.
413 Deseille, "Hesychast Prayer in the Orthodox Church", p. 245.
414 Jim Forest, *Praying with Icons* (Maryknoll, NY: Orbis, 2006), p. 15.
415 Ware, *The Jesus Prayer*, pp. 9–10.
416 Deseille, "Hesychast Prayer in the Orthodox Church", p. 253.
417 Gillet, *On the Invocation of the Name of Jesus*, p. 36.
418 Gillet, *On the Invocation of the Name of Jesus*, pp. 21–2.
419 Gillet, *On the Invocation of the Name of Jesus*, p. 91.
420 Ware, *The Power of the Name*, pp. 6–7.
421 Deseille, "Hesychast Prayer in the Orthodox Church", p. 250.
422 Hierotheos Vlachos, *A Night in the Desert of the Holy Mountain: Discussion with a Hermit on the Jesus Prayer*, tr. Effie Mavromichali (Levadia, Greece: Birth of the Theotokos Monastery, 2009), pp. 166–7.

423 Ignatius Brianchaninov, *On the Prayer of Jesus*, tr. Fr Lazarus (Boston, MA: New Seeds Books, 2006), p. 3.
424 Brianchaninov, *On the Prayer of Jesus*, pp. 41–5.
425 Brianchaninov, *On the Prayer of Jesus*, p. 50.
426 Brianchaninov, *On the Prayer of Jesus*, p. 62.
427 Brianchaninov, *On the Prayer of Jesus*, p. 96.
428 Brianchaninov, *On the Prayer of Jesus*, pp. 50, 62.
429 Brianchaninov, *On the Prayer of Jesus*, pp. 72–5.
430 Vlachos, *A Night in the Desert of the Holy Mountain*.
431 Vlachos, *A Night in the Desert of the Holy Mountain*, p. 169.
432 Kyriakos Markides, *Inner River: A Pilgrimage to the Heart of Christian Spirituality* (New York: Image Books, 2012), pp. 281–307.
433 Markides, *Inner River*, p. 284.
434 Markides, *Inner River*, p. 291.
435 Brianchaninov, *On the Prayer of Jesus*, p. 96.
436 Sakharov, *On Prayer*, p. 143.
437 Sakharov, *On Prayer*, pp. 142–6.
438 Sakharov, *On Prayer*, pp. 15–16.
439 St John Climacus, *The Ladder of Divine Ascent*, tr. Colm Luibheid and Norman Russell (Mahwah, NJ: Paulist Press, 1982), p. 200.
440 St John Climacus, *The Ladder of Divine Ascent*, p. 270.
441 St John Climacus, *The Ladder of Divine Ascent*, p. 276.
442 St John Climacus, *The Ladder of Divine Ascent*, p. 112.
443 Ware, *The Power of the Name*, p. 29.
444 Ware, *The Power of the Name*, p. 30.
445 Deseille, "Hesychast Prayer in the Orthodox Church", p. 233.
446 Deseille, "Hesychast Prayer in the Orthodox Church", p. 235.
447 Deseille, "Hesychast Prayer in the Orthodox Church", pp. 239–40.
448 Deseille, "Hesychast Prayer in the Orthodox Church", p. 246.
449 Ware, *The Power of the Name*, pp. 19–23.
450 Anthony Golynsky-Mihailovsky, *Two Elders on the Jesus Prayer*, ed. and comp. N. M. Novikov and tr. Igor V. Ksenzov (Hayesville, OH: Skete of the Entrance of the Theotokos into the Temple, 2008).
451 Golynsky-Michailovsky, *Two Elders*, p. 31.
452 Golynsky-Michailovsky, *Two Elders*, p. 43.
453 Golynsky-Michailovsky, *Two Elders*, p. 76.

454 Sakharov, *On Prayer*, p. 143.
455 Frederica Mathewes-Green, *The Jesus Prayer: The Ancient Desert Prayer that Tunes the Heart to God* (Brewster, MA: Paraclete Press, 2009).
456 Simon Barrington-Ward, *The Jesus Prayer: A Way to Contemplation* (Boston, MA: Pauline Books, 2011) and Simon Barrington-Ward & Brother Ramon, *Praying the Jesus Prayer Together* (Peabody, MA: Hendrickson Publishers, 2004).
457 Lev Gillet (A Monk of the Eastern Church), *On the Invocation of the Name of Jesus* (Springfield, IL: Templegate Publishers, 1985) and George Maloney SJ, *Prayer of the Heart* (Notre Dame, IN: Ave Maria Press, 1981).
458 Adolphe Franck, *The Kabbalah: The Religious Philosophy of the Hebrews* (Secaucus, NJ: Citadel Press, 1967), pp. 16–18.
459 Seraphim Rose, *Orthodoxy and the Religion of the Future* (Platina, California: Saint Herman of Alaska Brotherhood, 2004), pp. 143–6.
460 James F. Wellington, *Christe Eleison! The Invocation of Christ in Eastern Monastic Psalmody c. 350–450* (Bern: Peter Lang, 2014), pp. 219–21.
461 Michael Delmonte, "Mantras and Meditation", *Perceptual and Motor Skills* 57 (1983), pp. 64–6.
462 Arraj, James and St. Romain, Philip, "John Main's Christian Meditation", in James Arraj and Philip St. Romain (eds), *Critical Questions in Christian Contemplative Practice* (Midland, OR: Inner Growth Books, 2007), pp. 8–15.
463 Arraj and St. Romain, "John Main's Christian Meditation", p. 11.
464 Brother Max Sculley DLS, "Christian Meditation: Pseudo-Contemplation", <http://www.christendom-awake.org/pages/book-promotions/yoga-tai-chi&reiki/cmpseudo.htm>, accessed 11 March 2018.
465 Connie Rossini, *Is Centering Prayer Catholic? Fr Thomas Keating Meets St Teresa of Avila and the CDF* (New Ulm, MN: Four Waters Press, 2015).
466 James Arraj, *From St John of the Cross to Us: The Story of a 400 Year Long Misunderstanding and What it Means for the Future of Christian Mysticism* (Chiloquin, OR: Inner Growth Books, 1999).
467 Arraj, *From St John of the Cross to Us*, p. 18.
468 St John of the Cross, *The Dark Night*, p. 317.
469 Teresa of Avila, *The Way of Perfection*, p. 300.
470 Teresa of Avila, *The Interior Castle*, p. 328.
471 Teresa of Avila, *The Interior Castle*, p. 329.
472 Teresa of Avila, *The Interior Castle*, p. 329.

[473] Teresa of Avila, *The Interior Castle*, p. 330.
[474] Arraj, *From St John of the Cross to Us*, p. 238.
[475] Arraj, *From St John of the Cross to Us*, pp. 235–40.
[476] Arraj, *From St John of the Cross to Us*, p. 235.
[477] Arraj, *From St John of the Cross to Us*, p. 237.
[478] Arraj, *From St John of the Cross to Us*, p. 240.
[479] William Meissner SJ, *Ignatius of Loyola: The Psychology of a Saint* (New York: Yale University Press, 1992).
[480] William Johnston, *Mystical Journey: An Autobiography* (Maryknoll, NY: Orbis, 2006), pp. 170–93.
[481] Philip St. Romain, *The Kundalini Process: A Christian Perspective* (Bel Aire, KS: Lulu Press, 2017).
[482] Henri Ellenberger, *The Discovery of the Unconscious: The History and Evolution of Dynamic Psychiatry* (New York: Basic Books, 1970), pp. 889–91.
[483] Christina and Stanislav Grof, *The Stormy Search for the Self: A Guide to Personal Growth through Transformational Crisis* (New York: Tarcher/Putnam Books, 1990).
[484] Ignatius of Loyola, "Rules for Discernment, First Set, Tenth Rule", in *The Spiritual Exercises of Saint Ignatius of Loyola*, tr. Michael Ivens SJ (London: Gracewing, 2004), p. 97.
[485] Dionysios Farasiotis, *The Gurus, the Young Man and Elder Paisios* (Platina, California: St Herman of Alaska Brotherhood, 2008).
[486] Klaus Kenneth, *Born to Hate, Reborn to Love: A Spiritual Odyssey from Head to Heart* (Dalton, PA: Mount Thabor Publishing, 2012).
[487] Rose, *Orthodoxy and the Religion of the Future*, pp. 67–9.
[488] *The Orthodox Study Bible* (Nashville, TN: Thomas Nelson Inc., 2008), p. 746.
[489] Rose, *Orthodoxy and the Religion of the Future*, pp. 45–51.
[490] William Johnston, in *The Cloud of Unknowing* and *The Book of Privy Counselling*, tr. and ed. William Johnston (New York: Image, 2014), p. 14.
[491] Johnston, in *The Cloud*, pp. 15–17.
[492] Sakharov, *On Prayer*, pp. 121–75.
[493] Sakharov, *On Prayer*, p. 124.
[494] Sakharov, *On Prayer*, pp. 133–4.
[495] Sakharov, *On Prayer*, p. 139.
[496] Sakharov, *On Prayer*, pp. 143–4.
[497] Sakharov, *On Prayer*, pp. 152–7.

⁴⁹⁸ Sakharov, *On Prayer*, p. 169.
⁴⁹⁹ John Meyendorff, *Christ in Eastern Christian Thought* (Crestwood, New York: St Vladimir's Seminary Press, 1975), pp. 128-9.
⁵⁰⁰ Ware, *The Power of the Name*, p. 4.
⁵⁰¹ Congregation for the Doctrine of the Faith, *Letter to the Bishops of the Catholic Church on some Aspects of Christian Meditation* (15 October 1989), <http://www.vatican.va/roman_curia/congregations/cfaith/documents/rc_con_cfaith_doc_19891015_meditazione-cristiana_en.html>, accessed 28 May 2019.
⁵⁰² Congregation for the Doctrine of the Faith, *Letter to the Bishops* I.2.
⁵⁰³ Congregation for the Doctrine of the Faith, *Letter to the Bishops* I.3.
⁵⁰⁴ Congregation for the Doctrine of the Faith, *Letter to the Bishops* III.8-9.
⁵⁰⁵ Congregation for the Doctrine of the Faith, *Letter to the Bishops* III.12.
⁵⁰⁶ Congregation for the Doctrine of the Faith, *Letter to the Bishops* IV.14.
⁵⁰⁷ Congregation for the Doctrine of the Faith, *Letter to the Bishops* IV.15.
⁵⁰⁸ Congregation for the Doctrine of the Faith, *Letter to the Bishops* V.16.
⁵⁰⁹ Congregation for the Doctrine of the Faith, *Letter to the Bishops* V.18.
⁵¹⁰ Congregation for the Doctrine of the Faith, *Letter to the Bishops* V.20.
⁵¹¹ Congregation for the Doctrine of the Faith, *Letter to the Bishops* V.23.
⁵¹² Congregation for the Doctrine of the Faith, *Letter to the Bishops* VI.26.
⁵¹³ Congregation for the Doctrine of the Faith, *Letter to the Bishops* VI.27.
⁵¹⁴ Congregation for the Doctrine of the Faith, *Letter to the Bishops* VI.28.
⁵¹⁵ Congregation for the Doctrine of the Faith, *Letter to the Bishops* VII.29.
⁵¹⁶ Congregation for the Doctrine of the Faith, *Letter to the Bishops* VII.30.
⁵¹⁷ Congregation for the Doctrine of the Faith, *Letter to the Bishops* VII.31.
⁵¹⁸ Bourgeault, *Centering Prayer and Inner Awakening*, pp. 70-1.
⁵¹⁹ John Cassian, *Conferences*, p. 138.
⁵²⁰ Congregation for the Doctrine of the Faith, *Letter to the Bishops* V.16.
⁵²¹ William Johnston, in *The Cloud of Unknowing* and *The Book of Privy Counselling*, trans. and ed. by William Johnston (New York: Image Books, 2014), p. 28.
⁵²² Sakharov, *On Prayer*, p. 168.
⁵²³ Sakharov, *On Prayer*, p. 168.
⁵²⁴ Sakharov, *On Prayer*, p. 169.
⁵²⁵ Constantine Tsirpanlis, *Introduction to Eastern Patristic Thought and Orthodox Theology* (Collegeville, MN: Liturgical Press, 1991), p. 34.

[526] Jean-Yves Leloup, *Being Still: Reflections on an Ancient Mystical Tradition*, tr. M. S. Laird (Mahwah, NJ: Paulist Press, 2003), pp. 1–12.
[527] John Climacus, *Ladder of Divine Ascent*, pp. 200, 270 and 276.
[528] Michael Casey, *Strangers to the City: Reflections on the Beliefs and Values of the Rule of Saint Benedict* (Brewster, MA: Paraclete Press, 2013), p. 167.
[529] Casey, *Strangers to the City*, p. 166.
[530] St Seraphim of Sarov, in *The Life and Teachings of Saint Seraphim of Sarov*, by N. Puretzki and the Monastery of Sarov (The Hague: Gozalov Books, 2008), p. 41.
[531] Sophrony Sakharov, *His Life is Mine*, tr. Rosemary Edmonds (Crestwood, NY: St Vladimir's Seminary Press, 1977), p. 120.

EU GPSR Authorized Representative:

LOGOS EUROPE, 9 rue Nicolas Poussin, 17000 La Rochelle, France

contact@logoseurope.eu

www.ingramcontent.com/pod-product-compliance
Lightning Source LLC
Chambersburg PA
CBHW071421160426
43195CB00013B/1764